At Issue

Foreign Oil Dependence

WITHDRAWN

Other Books in the At Issue Series:

Are Adoption Policies Fair?

Do Veterans Receive Adequate Health Care?

Guns and Crime

Has No Child Left Behind Been Good for Education?

How Does Advertising Impact Teen Behavior?

How Should the U.S. Proceed in Iraq?

National Security

Reality TV

Senior Citizens and Driving

Should Cameras Be Allowed in Courtrooms?

Should Drilling Be Permitted in the Arctic National Wildlife Refuge?

Should Governments Negotiate with Terrorists?

Should Juveniles Be Tried as Adults?

Should the Legal Drinking Age Be Lowered?

Should Parents Be Allowed to Choose the Gender of Their Children?

Should Social Networking Sites Be Banned?

Teen Driving

What Is the Future of the U.S. Economy?

At Issue

Foreign Oil Dependence

Susan C. Hunnicutt, Book Editor

GREENHAVEN PRESS

A part of Gale, Cengage Learning

GALE
CENGAGE Learning

Detroit • New York • San Francisco • New Haven, Conn • Waterville, Maine • London

Christine Nasso, *Publisher*
Elizabeth Des Chenes, *Managing Editor*

© 2008 Greenhaven Press, a part of Gale, Cengage Learning.

Gale and Greenhaven Press are registered trademarks used herein under license.

For more information, contact:
Greenhaven Press
27500 Drake Rd.
Farmington Hills, MI 48331-3535
Or you can visit our Internet site at gale.cengage.com

For product information and technology assistance, contact us at

Gale Customer Support, 1-800-877-4253
For permission to use material from this text or product, submit all requests online at
www.cengage.com/permissions

Further permissions questions can be emailed to permissionrequest@cengage.com

Articles in Greenhaven Press anthologies are often edited for length to meet page requirements. In addition, original titles of these works are changed to clearly present the main thesis and to explicitly indicate the author's opinion. Every effort is made to ensure that Greenhaven Press accurately reflects the original intent of the authors. Every effort has been made to trace the owners of copyrighted material.

Cover photograph reproduced by permission of © Images.com/Corbis.

LIBRARY OF CONGRESS CATALOGING-IN-PUBLICATION DATA

Foreign oil dependence / Susan C. Hunnicutt, book editor.
    p. cm. -- (At issue)
  Includes bibliographical references and index.
  ISBN-13: 978-0-7377-4060-8 (hardcover)
  ISBN-10: 0-7377-4060-4 (hardcover)
  ISBN-13: 978-0-7377-4061-5 (pbk.)
  ISBN-10: 0-7377-4061-2 (pbk.)
  1. Petroleum industry and trade--Government policy--United States. 2. Petroleum industry and trade--Political aspects--United States. 3. Energy policy--United States. 4. Petroleum conservation--United States. I. Hunnicutt, Susan
  HD9566.F672 2008
  333.8'2320973--dc22

            2007050858

Printed in the United States of America
1 2 3 4 5   12 11 10 09 08

ED345

Contents

Introduction   7

1. Good Energy Policy Is the Key to   11
   America's Energy Future
   Barack Obama

2. Government Interference in the   22
   Energy Industry Is Bad Policy
   Ben Lieberman

3. Energy Independence Is a Worthwhile   27
   and Achievable Goal
   Patrick Mazza and Rich Feldman

4. Energy Independence Is a Misguided   33
   and Unrealistic Goal
   Julia A. Seymour

5. Dependence On Oil Threatens America's Interests   40
   Frederick W. Smith and P.X. Kelley

6. Dependence On Oil Is Not a Threat   44
   to National Security
   Shikha Dalmia

7. Good Relations with Venezuela Is the Key   48
   to U.S. Energy Security
   Bernardo Alvarez

8. The United States Should Not Seek   53
   to Control Iraqi Oil
   Jerry M. Landay

9. The United States Should Be More Involved   57
   in Iraqi Oil Development
   Michael Makovsky

10. Coal Is the Key to America's Energy Future   **63**
   Craig Thomas

11. Coal-Based Energy Independence Threatens   **66**
   the Environment
   Bradford Plumer

12. Using Home-Grown Ethanol Can Contribute   **71**
   to Energy Independence
   Joel Makower

13. Ethanol Will Not Contribute to   **76**
   U.S. Energy Independence
   Robert Bryce

14. Energy-Efficient Transportation Can   **86**
   Reduce America's Foreign Oil Dependence
   Chris Wolf

Organizations to Contact   **90**

Bibliography   **94**

Index   **100**

Introduction

In 2006 Michael W. Wynne, the secretary of the air force for the George W. Bush administration, told a colleague it was essential for the air force to develop a plan "to wean us off oil." He subsequently drafted a letter to air force servicepeople in which he said that "moving toward energy independence is a critical element to ensuring U.S. economic and national security in the long run." As Wynne explained in his letter, every $10 increase in the cost of a barrel of oil results in an additional $600 million a year in mission-related expenses for the air force. As the person responsible for organizing, training, and equipping the air force and assuring that it meets its current and future operational requirements, Wynne was aware of how costly U.S. dependence on foreign oil has become. The air force is the Department of Defense's (DoD) largest consumer of energy, with an annual energy bill that totaled $6.7 billion in 2006. The air force mobility fleet, which transports people and supplies around the globe, accounts for 42 percent of total DoD energy costs. Eighty percent of the air force's fuel costs are for aviation activities, including training, exercises, and deployments.

As a result of increased concern about the impact of rising oil prices on military preparedness, the air force has begun experimenting with replacing JP-8, a petroleum-based jet fuel that has been the standard since the mid-1990s, with synthetic fuel blends that can be produced in part from domestic coal or shale oil.

Concerns about the national security implications of the U.S. appetite for oil have been steadily increasing in recent years. The need for a comprehensive energy policy was an issue in the 2000 election, when George Bush criticized the Bill Clinton administration for weakening the nation by increasing U.S. dependence on foreign oil, including Iraqi oil. At that time, the Bush campaign also advocated for trade policies that would increase U.S. access to foreign oil supplies. Nevertheless, the question Bush raised in the 2000 campaign about whether U.S. reliance on foreign oil is a threat to national security has not gone away. Rather, as the energy crisis faced by the U.S. Air Force demonstrates, it has become more persistent in recent years.

In 2005 the White House published a fact sheet, "Promoting Energy Independence and Security," that outlined five initiatives to make more efficient use of existing energy resources and to develop new sources of energy. In addition to facilitating the licensing of new nuclear plants, simplifying regulations to increase U.S. petroleum refining capacity, and clarifying rules governing the building of liquefied natural gas terminals, Bush administration proposals included tax credits for energy-efficient vehicles and the development of clean-energy technologies. "Our growing economy requires affordable, reliable, and secure supplies of energy," the fact sheet stated.

Not everyone agrees that energy independence is a rational goal, however, or one that will lead to greater security for the United States. "Petroleum prices everywhere are set in a world market," Pietro S. Nivola, a Senior Fellow at the Brookings Institution, argued in a 2002 article on the American Petroleum Institute Web site. Since price increases overseas inevitably result in increased prices for domestic energy supplies, regardless of the source, Nivola reasoned, there is very little that individual nations, even large nations, can do to insulate themselves from increases in the price of oil produced overseas. In his article, Nivola suggested that the self-sufficiency or energy independence model that has at times been proposed by President Bush is "fundamentally flawed." He criticized the White House for "rhapsodiz[ing] about bygone days" when America was less reliant on foreign oil.

Shikha Dalmia, writing more recently for the libertarian Reason Foundation, takes a similar position: The global demand for oil has synchronized prices around the world, making energy independence an unrealistic goal, he argues. "War or peace, no amount of domestic production will give us 'independence' from the law of supply and demand," he concludes. Dalmia goes even further, though. He argues that U.S. reliance on foreign oil, far from threatening national security, is actually a source of international stability. "Our dependence on foreign oil is only the flip side of their dependence on our purchases," he notes. "The mutual dependence that trade breeds fosters peace because it gives hostile trading partners an incentive to refrain from acting on their hostility."

New York Times columnist Thomas L. Friedman, who has written extensively on the economic and cultural implications of the new global economy, agrees about the interconnectedness of international oil markets. He judges the political consequences of embracing energy interdependence differently, however. He has coined a term—*petrolism*—that casts oil-based interdependence in a less positive light. Petrolism is "the politics of using oil income to buy off one's citizens with subsidies and government jobs, using oil and gas exports to intimidate or buy off one's enemies, and using oil profits to build up one's internal security forces and army to keep oneself ensconced in power, without any transparency or checks and balances."

Friedman has argued that there are other reasons, not purely economic, why the United States should struggle to overcome its addiction to oil. As he sees it, high oil prices ($60 a barrel when he wrote his column in 2006, more than $90 a barrel as of this writing) generate such enormous amounts of wealth that they inevitably breed authoritarianism and have a corrupting effect on democratic institutions. Anti-democratic regimes like those in Russia, Nigeria, Sudan, Iran, and Central Asia thrive on high oil prices, he notes. According to Friedman, the demand for oil that is generated by what he calls the U.S. addiction to oil has been the cause of similar democratic failures around the world. Leaders who have easy access to oil wells and easy access to international markets never have to "tap their people's energy and creativity," he argues. The result is that "politics in a petrolist state is not about building a society or an educational system that maximizes its people's ability to innovate, export and compete. It is simply about who controls the oil tap."

Furthermore, Friedman argues, violent Islamism feeds off the authoritarianism of petrolist regimes in the Middle East. In this way petrolism—and American oil dollars spent overseas—fuels terrorism. "We need a president and a Congress with the guts not just to invade Iraq," Friedman writes, "but also to impose a gasoline tax and inspire conservation at home." In Friedman's view, a green energy policy with significant long-term incentives for the development of wind and solar power and biofuels is needed to free the United States from its need to make large purchases of oil abroad, thereby unwittingly lending support to antidemocratic regimes.

As these differing perspectives demonstrate, U.S. dependence on foreign oil is a complex, multifaceted, and often controversial subject. Is U.S. dependence on foreign oil a key element in its economic success, or is it damaging to the long-term interests of the United States, including its military interests? Should the United States as a whole, and not just the air force, focus on developing domestic energy supplies and wean itself from its need to purchase oil overseas? What role should the government play in setting energy policy? Do the commercial relationships engendered by the need for energy promote international stability, or do they fuel terrorism? These are some of the questions that are explored in *At Issue: Foreign Oil Dependence*.

1

Good Energy Policy Is the Key to America's Energy Future

Barack Obama

Barack Obama is a U.S. Senator from Illinois and a Democratic candidate in the 2008 presidential race.

The United States depends on oil for more than 96% of its transportation needs, yet we have only 3% of the world's oil reserves. The result is that we have become dependent on and vulnerable to people who are our enemies, who know they can use oil as a weapon against us. Energy security has become the most important national security issue. We can fight the war on terror by building fuel-efficient cars that are less dependent on oil and by developing alternative energy sources, such as ethanol, that are renewable and can be grown in the United States.

In this year's [2006] State of the Union address, President [George W.] Bush told us that it was time to get serious about America's addiction to foreign oil. The next day, we found out that his idea didn't sit too well with the Saudi Royal Family. A few hours later, Energy Secretary Bodman backtracked and assured the world that even though the President said he planned to reduce the amount of oil we import from the Middle East, he actually didn't mean that literally.

If there's a single example out there that encapsulates the ability of unstable, undemocratic governments to wield undue influence over America's national security just because of our dependence on oil, this is it.

Barack Obama, Governor's Ethanol Coalition, Washington, DC, February 28, 2006.
http://www.barackobama.com/2006/02/28/energy_security_is_national_se.php.

Now, I could stand up here and give you all plenty of reasons why it's a good idea for this country to move away from an oil-based economy. I could cite studies from scientists and experts and even our own State Department detailing the dangers of global warming—how it can destroy our coastal areas and generate more deadly storms. I could talk forever about the economic consequences of dependence—how it's decimating our auto industry and costing us jobs and emptying our wallets at the pump. And I could talk about the millions of new jobs and entire new industries we could create by transitioning to an alternative-fuel economy.

In the Words of Our Enemies

But all we really need to know about the danger of our oil addiction comes directly from the mouths of our enemies:

"[Oil] is the umbilical cord and lifeline of the crusader community." These are the words of Al Qaeda.

"Focus your operations on oil, especially in Iraq and the Gulf area, since this will cause them to die off [on their own]." These are the words of Osama bin Laden.

More than anything else, these comments represent a realization of American weakness shared by the rest of the world. It's a realization that for all of our military might and economic dominance, the Achilles heel of the most powerful country on Earth is the oil we cannot live without.

Oil single-handedly fuels 96% of our transportation needs, and it's also critical to the manufacture of millions of goods and products in this country. As we saw during Hurricane Katrina, this kind of dependency means that the loss of even a small amount of oil and refining capacity for just a few days can cause economic panic and soaring prices. A serious embargo or permanent loss could cause untold disaster.

It would be nice if we could produce our way out of this problem, but it's just not possible. We only have 3% of the world's oil reserves. We could start drilling in ANWR [the

Arctic National Wildlife Refuge] today, and at its peak, which would be more than a decade from now, it would give us enough oil to take care of our transportation needs for about a month.

As a result, every single hour we spend $18 million on foreign oil. It doesn't matter if these countries are budding democracies, despotic regimes, or havens for the madrassas [Islamic religious schools] that plant the seeds of terror in young minds—they get our money because we need their oil.

One need only glance at headlines around the world to understand how dangerous this addictive arrangement truly is.

In Iran, Islamic fundamentalists are forging ahead with their nuclear program, knowing full well that the world's response to their actions will be influenced by our need for their oil. In fact, reports of a $100 billion oil deal between Iran and China were soon followed by China's refusal to press for sanctions against Iran over its nuclear intentions.

In Nigeria, militant rebels have been attacking the country's oil pipelines in recent weeks, sending prices soaring and calling into question the political stability of a country that represents America's fifth-largest source of oil imports.

In Saudi Arabia, Al Qaeda has been attempting attacks on that country's poorly defended oil refineries for years. On Friday, they almost succeeded as a truck full of explosives was detonated by the shots of security guards just before it entered the refinery. Even this minor damage caused oil prices to jump $2 in a single day. But a former CIA agent tells us that if terrorists ever succeeded in destroying an entire oil complex, it could take enough oil off the market to cause economic catastrophe in the United States.

Oil Is a Weapon

Our enemies are fully aware that they can use oil as a weapon against America. And if we don't take this threat as seriously as the bombs they build or the guns they buy, we will be fighting the War on Terror with one hand tied behind our back.

Now, the good news about the President's decision to finally focus on energy independence after five years is that it helps build bipartisan consensus that our reliance on foreign oil is a problem and shows that he understands the potential of renewable fuels to make a difference.

The bad news is that the President's energy policy treats our dependence on oil as more of a nuisance than a serious threat.

Just one day after he told us in the State of the Union that renewable fuels were the key to an energy independent future, we learned that the President's budget cuts would force layoffs at the National Renewable Energy Laboratory. [A few weeks later,] this made for a rather awkward situation when the President wanted to use the lab for a photo-op—so awkward that the White House actually re-hired the laid-off researchers just to avoid the embarrassment.

This is only one example, but it tells the story of a larger weakness in the President's energy policy: it's simply not commensurate to the challenge.

There's a reason that some have compared the quest for energy independence to the Manhattan Project or the Apollo moon landing. Like those historic efforts, moving away from an oil economy is a major challenge that will require a sustained national commitment.

During World War II, we had an entire country working around the clock to produce enough planes and tanks to beat the Axis powers. In the middle of the Cold War, we built a national highway system so we had a quick way to transport military equipment across the country. When we wanted to beat the Russians into space, we poured millions into a national education initiative that graduated thousands of new scientists and engineers.

Commitment Is Required

If we hope to strengthen our security and control our own foreign policy, we can offer no less of a commitment to energy independence.

But so far, President Bush seems like he is offering less—much less.

His funding for renewable fuels is at the same level it was the day he took office.

He refuses to call for even a modest increase in fuel-efficiency standards for cars and trucks.

His latest budget funds less then half of the energy bill he himself signed into law—leaving hundreds of millions of dollars in under-funded energy proposals.

And while he cannot seem to find the funding for any of these energy proposals, he has no problem allowing the oil companies to stiff taxpayers $7 billion in royalties that they owe us for drilling on public lands. These are the same oil companies that are currently enjoying the highest profits on record.

Again, this is just not a serious commitment to energy independence. The solutions are too timid—the reforms too small. America's dependence on oil is a major threat to our national security, and the American people deserve a bold commitment that has the full force of their government behind it.

This isn't to lay the blame for our energy problems entirely at the feet of our President. This is an issue that politicians from both parties clamor about when gas prices are the headline of the month, only to fall back into a trance of inaction once things calm down. And so we all need to get serious here. Automakers need to get serious about shifting their technology to greater fuel-efficiency, consumers need to get serious about buying hybrid cars, and Washington needs to get serious about working together to find a real solution to our energy crisis.

Such a solution is not only possible, it's already being implemented in other places around the world. Countries like Japan are creating jobs and slowing oil consumption by churning out and buying millions of fuel-efficient cars. Brazil, a nation that once relied on foreign countries to import 80% of its crude oil, will now be entirely self-sufficient in a few years thanks to its investment in biofuels.

So why can't we do this? Why can't we make energy security one of the great American projects of the 21st century?

With technology we have on the shelves right now and fuels we can grow right here in America, by 2025 we can reduce our oil imports by over 7.5 million barrels per day.

We Can Do Better

The answer is, we can. The President's energy proposal would reduce our oil imports by 4.5 million barrels per day by 2025. Not only can we do better than that, we must do better than that if we hope to make a real dent in our oil dependency. With technology we have on the shelves right now and fuels we can grow right here in America, by 2025 we can reduce our oil imports by over 7.5 million barrels per day—an amount greater than all the oil we are expected to import from the entire Middle East.

We can do this by focusing on two things: the cars we drive and the fuels we use.

First, the cars. For years, we've hesitated to raise fuel economy standards as a nation in part because of a very legitimate concern—the impact it would have on Detroit. The auto industry is right when they argue that transitioning to more hybrid and fuel-efficient cars would require massive investment at a time when they're struggling under the weight of rising health care costs, sagging profits, and stiff competition.

But it's precisely because of that competition that they don't have a choice. China now has a higher fuel economy standard than we do, and Japan's Toyota is doubling production of the popular Prius to sell 100,000 in the U.S. [in 2006].

There is now no doubt that fuel-efficient cars represent the future of the auto industry. If American car companies hope to be a part of that future—if they hope to survive—they must start building more of these cars.

But that's not to say we should leave the industry to face these costs on its own. Yes, we should raise fuel economy standards by 3% a year over the next fifteen years, starting in 2008. With the technology they already have, this should be an achievable goal for automakers. But we can help them get there.

Right now, one of the biggest costs facing auto manufacturers isn't the cars they make, it's the health care they provide. Health care costs make up $1,500 of the price of every GM [General Motors] car that's made—more than the cost of steel. Retiree health care alone cost the Big 3 automakers nearly $6.7 billion just [in 2005].

Let's Make a Deal

So here's the deal we can make with the auto companies. It's a piece of legislation I introduced called "Health Care for Hybrids," and it would allow the federal government to pick up part of the tab for the auto companies' retiree health care costs. In exchange, the auto companies would then use some of that savings to build and invest in more fuel-efficient cars. It's a win-win proposal for the industry—their retirees will be taken care of, they'll save money on health care, and they'll be free to invest in the kind of fuel-efficient cars that are the key to their competitive future.

Now, building cars that use less oil is only one side of the equation. The other involves replacing the oil we use with home-grown biofuels. The Governors in this room have long known about this potential, and all of you have been leading the way on ethanol in your own states.

This coalition also knows that corn-based ethanol is only the beginning. If we truly want to harness the power of these fuels and the promise of this market, we can and must generate more cellulosic ethanol from agricultural products like corn stocks, switch grass and other crops our farmers grow.

Already, there are hundreds of fueling stations that use a blend of ethanol and gasoline known as E85, and there are millions of cars on the road with the flexible-fuel tanks necessary to use this fuel—including my own.

But the challenge we face with these biofuels is getting them out of the labs, out of the farms, and onto the wider commercial market. Every scientific study in the world could sing the praises of biofuels, but you might still be hard-pressed to find an investor willing to take the risk on a cellulosic ethanol plant or a brand-name petroleum company willing to build an E85 fueling station.

Washington should lead the way on energy independency by making sure that every single automobile the government purchases is a flexible-fuel vehicle.

The federal government can help in two ways here. First, we can reduce the risk of investing. We already do this in a number of ways by funding projects critical to our national security. Energy independence should be no different. By developing an Energy Technology Program at the Defense Department, we can provide loan guarantees and venture capital to those with the best plans to develop and sell biofuels on a commercial market. The Defense Department will also hold a competition where private corporations get funding to see who can build the best new alternative-fuel plant. The Department can then use these new technologies to improve the energy security of our own military.

A Market for Renewable Fuels

Once we take the risk out of investing, the second thing the government can do is to let the private sector know that there will always be a market for renewable fuels. We can do this in a few ways.

First, we should ramp up the renewable fuel standard and create an alternative diesel standard in this country so that by 2025, 65 billion gallons of alternative fuels per year will be blended into the petroleum supply.

Second, Washington should lead the way on energy independency by making sure that every single automobile the government purchases is a flexible-fuel vehicle—starting today. When it becomes possible in the coming years, we should make sure that every government car is a plug-in hybrid as well.

Third, I'm supporting legislation that would make sure every single new car in America is a flexible-fuel vehicle within a decade. Currently it costs manufacturers just $100 to add these tanks to each car. But we can do them one better. If they install flexible-fuel tanks in their cars before the decade's up, the government should provide them a $100 tax credit to do it—so there's no excuse for delay.

Fourth, there are already millions of people driving flexible-fuel vehicles who don't know it. The auto companies shouldn't get CAFE [Corporate Average Fuel Economy] credit for making these cars if they don't let buyers know about them, so I'd like to ask the industry to follow GM's lead and put a yellow gas cap on all flexible- fuel vehicles starting today. Also, they should send a letter to those people who already have flexible-fuel vehicles so they can start filling up their tank at the closest E85 station.

Finally, since there are only around 500 fueling stations that pump E85 in the country, we recently passed legislation that would provide tax credits of up to $30,000 for those who want to install E85 pumps at their station. But we should do even more—we should make sure that in the coming years, E85 stations are as easy to find as your gas station is now.

Make no mistake—none of these reforms will come easy, and they won't happen overnight. But we can't continue to settle for piecemeal, bite-sized solutions to our energy crisis. We need a national commitment to energy security, and to emphasize that commitment, we should install a Director of Energy Security to oversee all of our efforts. Like the Chairman of the Joint Chiefs and the National Intelligence Director, this person would be an advisor to the National Security Council and have the full authority to coordinate America's energy policy across all levels of government. He or she would approve all major budget decisions and provide a full report to Congress and the country every year detailing the progress we're making toward our 2025 goal.

Now is the time for serious leadership to get us started down the path of energy independence.

In the days and months after [the terrorist attacks of] September 11th, Americans were waiting to be called to something bigger than themselves. Just like their parents and grandparents of the Greatest Generation, they were willing to serve and defend their country—not only on the fields of war, but on the homefront too.

A Chance to Serve

This is our chance to step up and serve. The war against international terrorism has pitted us against a new kind of enemy that wages terror in new and unconventional ways. At home, fighting that enemy won't require us to build the massive war machine that Franklin Roosevelt called for so many years ago, but it will require us to harness our own renewable forms of energy so that oil can never be used as a weapon against America. From farmers and scientists to entrepreneurs and governors, everyone has a role to play in this effort. In fact . . . I'm sitting down with business and military leaders to discuss this very topic.

Now is the time for serious leadership to get us started down the path of energy independence. Now is the time for this call to arms. I hope some of the ideas I've laid out today can serve as a basis for this call, but I also hope that members of both parties and all levels of government can come together in the near future to launch this serious quest for energy independence.

2

Government Interference in the Energy Industry Is Bad Policy

Ben Lieberman

Ben Lieberman is affiliated with the Thomas A. Roe Institute for Economic Policy Studies at the Heritage Foundation in Washington, DC.

In his 2007 State of the Union address, President George W. Bush said that America is "addicted to oil." He proposed a number of policy changes, including replacing 20 percent of domestic gasoline supplies with renewable fuels. It would be bad policy for the government to exert this kind of control on the energy industry. The United States has substantial oil deposits that are off limits due to federal law. The best thing the president could do to increase U.S. energy independence would be to expand domestic exploration and production by removing federal constraints on these domestic oil reserves.

Those who trust the free market more than the government to address the nation's energy challenges have sometimes cringed during President Bush's past State of the Union addresses. Unfortunately, the 2007 address (and the supporting materials released beforehand) added to this tradition, though there were a few bright spots as well. Overall, the energy plan described in [2007's] State of the Union would lead to higher, not lower, energy prices for the American people.

Ben Lieberman, "State of the Union 2007: A Counterproductive Energy Policy," Web Memo, January 23, 2007. Reproduced by permission.

The Good

The President has not abandoned the single best energy idea Washington can undertake: expanding domestic oil and natural gas production. Recent Department of the Interior studies, conducted pursuant to the 2005 energy bill, confirm that the United States has substantial oil and natural gas deposits. These studies also show that much of these onshore and offshore resources are off-limits due to legal and regulatory constraints. In fact, America remains the only nation on earth that has restricted access to a substantial portion of its domestic energy potential. Removing the federal impediments on domestic exploration and drilling will allow for greater domestic supplies and potentially lower prices in the years ahead. Of course, the change in Congress makes passage of such measures unlikely, but it is important that the President has kept the domestic drilling debate alive.

The President also deserves credit for something he did not say: He did not announce a new program to cap fossil fuel use in order to fight climate change. Such a measure would do far more economic harm than environmental good.

The President is also to be commended for recognizing that urban traffic congestion is a significant cause of air pollution and wasted fuel and for proposing financial incentives for states and communities to remedy the problem. One important approach that several states have recently adopted to reduce congestion are "performance based" transportation policies that hold state and local transportation officials accountable for achieving quantitative measures of congestion relief. In Texas, for example, the state department of transportation is required to reduce congestion by 50 percent in 25 years, while the Georgia department of transportation is required to reduce Atlanta's Travel Time Index by a specified amount over the next several years. Several other states have implemented similar plans, and many more are in the development stage.

In implementing his proposals, the President should resist efforts to impose certain specific processes—such as congestion charges or expensive commuter transit systems—on communities. Instead, he should set specific quantitative goals for congestion mitigation and allow each community to determine the most cost effective way to achieve them.

The Bad

The biggest idea in the speech was also the worst, the so-called "Twenty in Ten" goal, which is the logical result of his announcement in last year's State of the Union Address that America is "addicted to oil." The President proposes to reduce domestic gasoline use by 20 percent in 10 years and would do this by mandating that 35 billion gallons of renewable fuels be used to fill the void. This is a big jump from the current renewables mandate of 4 billion gallons per year, which is set to increase to 7.5 billion in 2012.

The current mandate, met mostly by corn-based ethanol, is already proving to be expensive. Adding even small amounts of ethanol to gasoline adds several cents to the price at the pump, and the mandate has raised food prices as corn supplies are split between food and fuel needs. Absent big breakthroughs that make ethanol production much cheaper, Twenty in Ten could send pump prices far higher. . . .

For this reason, the President also promised more money for research into "cellulosic" ethanol, made from wood chips, grasses, or other plants materials instead of corn. The hope is that cheaper means of producing ethanol can supplement the corn-based variety and meet the 35 billion gallon target in a cost-effective manner. But cellulosic ethanol is far from viable at this point, and the track record for federally directed alternative energy research programs is not good. Most of the money for such programs has been wasted on boondoggles like the Carter-era Syn-fuels program, and cellulosic ethanol has all the hallmarks of being the next such Washington boondoggle. In addition, having the federal government direct the selection of new technology would have the effect of crowding out other promising technologies from being discovered and developed. Instead, the markets will respond to mandates and subsidies that reflect what Washington wants, rather than exploring breakthroughs not yet dreamed of.

The Twenty in Ten program and its 35-billion-gallon alternative energy mandate will likely be bad news for consumers. After all, the only reason these alternatives have to be mandated in the first place is that they are too expensive to compete otherwise. Twenty in Ten would force the American people to switch from less expensive gasoline to more expensive ethanol.

The President's push for tighter fuel economy standards for cars is also bad news for the American people.

Beyond costs, it is not even clear if a big boost in ethanol use would reduce energy imports much. When certain factors are taken into account—specifically, that ethanol reduces fuel economy by a third compared to gasoline and that substantial amounts of energy are consumed to produce it—its use does not provide the additional energy benefits proponents claim. This proposal is seemingly at odds with other energy goals the President laid out in his speech.

Growing America's way out of dependence on foreign oil makes for nice bipartisan-supported sound bites, and some version of this measure may pass, but the bottom line impact is very likely to be increases at the pump.

The President's push for tighter fuel economy standards for cars is also bad news for the American people. Fuel-efficient models, including a growing number of hybrids, are already available for those who want them. An overly stringent new fuel economy standard would only serve to force that choice on everyone. Granted, it is easy to calculate big "fuel savings" from forcing people into vehicles smaller than they prefer, but this is hardly what the American people want or need.

Ideas for Improvement

Generally speaking, the President's energy policy, as reflected in previous State of the Union addresses as well as this one, has drifted towards the same troubling approach Americans saw during the Carter Administration. President Carter thought that energy policy was something best managed by the federal government—Washington could dictate which types of energy to use and which not to use, what to use them for, and how much they should cost and commandeer private sector research and development programs. The result was a vicious circle of government bungling exacerbating problems—remember gas lines?—which led to new government bungling that made things worse. It ended only after [Ronald] Reagan took office and deregulated energy markets.

The President should take a less Carteresque and more Reaganesque tone on energy. Unleashing the free market by eliminating restrictions on drilling for domestic oil and gas is a good start. Streamlining regulations that hamper everything from refinery expansions to new coal and nuclear power plants is another. Removing restrictions on the much more efficient sugar cane ethanol imports is yet another. These and other free-market steps, however, will not be easy to enact in the current Congress and so vetoing bad energy bills may be the most important thing the President can do in the next two years. But instead of stopping the big government energy bandwagon, the President appears in many instances to be joining it.

3

Energy Independence Is a Worthwhile and Achievable Goal

Patrick Mazza and Rich Feldman

Patrick Mazza is research director for Climate Solutions, www .climatesolutions.org. Rich Feldman is a senior policy advisor for Seattle Mayor Greg Nickels, www.seattle.gov/mayor/. For more on the Apollo Alliance, visit www.apolloalliance.org.

Dependence on oil makes Americans vulnerable not only to severe weather events, but also to acts of violence in the Middle East. The state of Washington has been a leader in national efforts to reduce dependence on foreign oil by promoting development of renewable fuels. There is more that can be done, and many are calling for a detailed plan to achieve energy independence within a decade, like the plan in the 1960s to land an American on the moon within ten years. State leaders could set firm goals for reduction of foreign oil imports. They could promote investment in energy-saving transportation technologies such as flex-fuel vehicles, develop stronger public transportation systems, and increase research in the development of cellulosic ethanol.

An economic earthquake is poised to shake the globe. By making preparations now for a future of expensive world oil supplies, we can build an economy with a more resilient foundation for jobs and prosperity.

Patrick Mazza and Rich Feldman, "The Road to Independence," *Seattle Post Intelligencer*, July 2, 2006. Reproduced by permission of the authors.

As former Federal Reserve chief Alan Greenspan told the Senate Foreign Relations Committee in 2006, "Even before the devastating hurricanes of last summer, world oil markets had been subject to a degree of strain not experienced for a generation. Today . . . the buffer between supply and demand is much too small to absorb shutdowns of even a small part of the world's oil supply."

On the Edge of a Crisis

The American economy is now like a car without shock absorbers. The next hurricane that slams into the Gulf Coast could send prices up at the pump again. But the next car bomb that successfully explodes at a major Saudi oil facility could send fuel pump prices above $5 or $6 per gallon. A doubling of oil prices from such a shock could cause a 2-5 percent slump in GDP, for one of the worst recessions since World War II.

While U.S. energy policy has seemed like a deer petrified in the headlights of oncoming calamity, leaders spanning the spectrum are now moving serious proposals for greater energy self-reliance. Just as President Kennedy challenged out nation to land on the moon within a decade, citizens across the country—trade unionists, farmers, security hawks, entrepreneurs, and state and local officials—are by word and deed challenging our nation to implement a new Apollo Project—to achieve clean energy independence within a decade. The farmer led 25x25 movement is calling for agriculture to produce 25% of U.S. energy by 2025. Bipartisan federal legislation aims to cut oil consumption seven million barrels by 2025.

Washington State has been a pioneer in these efforts. In 2006, Gov. Chris Gregoire united farmers, unions, environmentalists, Republicans, and Democrats to sign into law a bill sponsored by Rep Jenea Holmquist that sets a state-wide standard to promote renewable fuels to replace some of the gasoline we now import from the Middle East and other troubled regions. In 2003, Seattle Mayor Nickels developed and passed a Clean and Green Fleet plan, setting a goal of using the cleanest fuels and most fuel-efficient vehicles available. As a result, the City reduced fleet use of fossil fuels by 12% compared to 1999 levels, and increased use of biodiesel in the City fleet by 4.5 times since 2003. By the end of 2007, all of the City's diesel tanks will be filled with B20 or B40. In addition, since 2003, 78% of the City's new light-duty vehicle purchases have been hybrid or biodiesel vehicles.

There is more, however, that Washington state can do to help reduce oil use by a transportation system 97 percent dependent on oil. So doing, we can help lead America toward clean energy independence that protects our economy, our environment and our security. The following five-point plan could help us achieve that goal:

A Five-Point Plan for Independence

1. Set an oil savings goal. First, we should set an oil savings goal. A California plan targets a 15% lower oil use in 2020 than 2000. Senator Maria Cantwell has introduced legislation to reduce U.S. oil imports 40 percent below 2025 projections. Hawaii Gov. Linda Lingle is pushing to cut state oil imports by 2020. Washington consumes roughly 3.6 billion gallons of oil per year in transportation fuels, with a typical annual growth rate of 1.7 percent for the past 25 years. State leaders should set firm goals and dates, first to halt increasing oil use and then to significantly reduce it, appointing an Oil Savings Task Force to map strategies.

2. Promote vehicles that reduce oil use. Cost-effective, off-the-shelf motor vehicle technologies could improve fuel efficiency by 60 percent in 10 years without reducing vehicle size or weight, says the Union of Concerned Scientists. State and local governments can promote better

mileage by public fleet purchases, and tax and license fee incentives. Requiring replacement tires to be as efficient as new car tires can improve mileage by three percent. Public education on proper tire inflation could have a real impact.

3. At least 100,000 Washington motorists are driving flex fuel vehicles capable of running on home-grown "E85"—85% ethanol fuel—instead of gasoline, yet there is only one retail E85 fuel pump in the entire state. State and local governments can provide incentives for station operators to install E85 pumps and make sure their own flex fuel vehicles run on E85.

4. Build up transit and transit-friendly communities. Public transportation uses half the oil per passenger mile as cars and SUVs, reports the Center for Transportation Excellence. Investing in bus and rail transit systems that provide frequent, reliable service is vital. Building compact communities provides the population base that makes frequent transit service feasible. Smart transit-oriented development could reduce oil use up to 10 percent by 2020, a California Energy Commission study shows.

5. Commercialize advanced biofuels. Building on our Renewable Fuels Standard, Washington should invest in the R & D necessary to develop the next generation of biofuels—so-called "cellulosic ethanol" based on Washington's abundant supplies of plant waste from its farms, forests and municipalities as well as specialized crops such as switchgrass. New technologies will produce cellulosic biofuels at costs competitive with gasoline.

6. Washington State University calculates the state annually generates 15 million dry tons in cellulose wastes. With near future technologies each million tons could displace

50 million gallons of petroleum fuels. Washington also has 14 million acres of croplands. Crops such as switch-grass could displace 200 million gallons per million acres. While only a portion of those tons and acres will be practical for fuel production, these figures indicate massive prospects. State farmlands also can grow oil crops capable of producing at least 50 million gallons of biodiesel annually. And a substantial chunk of the $9 billion that we annually pay to oil companies will wind up in Washington farmer wallets.

7. Electrify transportation. Outcompeted by gasoline in the early days of the car, electricity is now returning in the form of gasoline-electric hybrids that significantly reduce fuel use. The next stage is the plug-in hybrid charged not only by car systems, but also by standard wall sockets.Because plug-ins run on electric charge longer than most people drive daily, liquid fuel use could drop as much as 85 percent. A Prius converted by Hymotion and tested by US Department of Energy's Idaho National Laboratory gets over 160 mpg of petroleum in the first 20 miles of urban driving while only using 3.3 kilowatts of electricity. A flex fuel plug-in car could be nearly oil free. Plug-In Partners is a national grass-roots initiative working to demonstrate to automakers that a market for flex fuel plug-ins exists today.

Plug-ins could make a big dent in global warming pollution. A UC Berkeley study shows that 500 kilowatt hours of electricity will replace one barrel of oil. Since plug-ins would be charged at night during off peak hours, they would rely on unused electrical generation capacity. Plug-ins could be virtually carbon free if Washington develops its significant undeveloped renewable power and energy efficiency resources. Passage of I-937, the Clean Energy Initiative in fall 2006, requiring the state meet 15 percent of its electricity needs with new renewables and efficiency, helps ensure that Washington taps its clean power potential. In addition, an Emissions Performance Standard that requires all new fossil electricity on the state grid meet minimum standards effectively locks new conventional coal plants out of the market.

A State Electrified Transportation Task Force could help advance demonstration projects and identify opportunities for state businesses in plug-in manufacture. Significant oil reductions can also be made by electrifying truck stops, and running port cranes and docked ships on electricity as is being done increasingly at our ports.

When America's founders came together at Independence Hall 230 years ago they knew it was time to take the future in their hands. We would either hang together or hang separately, they told each other. Now we are called to secure our independence from politically unstable regions and oil companies with a long record of resistance to alternatives. Disruptive oil shocks are barreling down on us. We will either hang economically as individuals or join in a bold agenda to replace petroleum fuels. Washington state has the public leadership, entrepreneurial vision and energy resources to lead this new American energy revolution. In upcoming elections citizens should ask candidates—What is your plan for dissolving the bonds of oil addiction and declaring clean energy independence?

4

Energy Independence Is a Misguided and Unrealistic Goal

Julia A. Seymour

Julia A. Seymour is an assistant editor and analyst for the Business and Media Institute of the Media Research Center in Alexandria, VA.

In spite of persistent calls for American energy independence, the United States is very self-reliant in its use of energy. If coal, nuclear, and renewable fuels are included, America is more than 70 percent energy independent. Canada and Mexico are the two largest sources of U.S. oil imports, and only 19 percent of imported oil comes from the Middle East. Support for energy independence is misguided because it results in higher taxes and costly subsidies for alternative energies, while providing no real cushion against disruptions in foreign oil supplies.

"[W]e have a serious problem. America is addicted to oil."

> *—President George W. Bush,*
> *2006 State of the Union address*

"For too long our nation has been dependent on foreign oil. . . . It is in our vital interest to diversify America's energy supply."

> *—President George W. Bush,*
> *2007 State of the Union address*

Julia A. Seymour, "Energy: Mission Impossible? Politicians and the Media Clamor for Energy Independence but Leave out Crucial Details," *Business & Media Institute*, January 24, 2007. Reproduced by permission.

It has figured prominently in the past two State of the Union speeches and has prompted waves of political and media support. But "energy independence" isn't a simple idea, nor is it a cheap one.

In 2006, it became a punchline for "Today Show" host Matt Lauer, who said, "I'm Matt, and I'm addicted to oil," during the NBC broadcast on Feb. 2, 2006.

What a difference a year makes. Now that leading Democrats and high-profile Republicans are all talking about "energy independence," the stakes for American energy producers and taxpayers are much higher. The topic was deemed "safe" for bipartisan discussion by ABC's Martha Raddatz on Nov. 9, 2006.

Journalists have been quick to press the idea. "Another question five years later, I think a lot of people thought in five years America would be energy independent or at least on its way to independence of the Middle East oil," Diane Sawyer asked Rudy Giuliani during ABC's "Good Morning America" on Sept. 11, 2006.

"Gas prices on the rise again. Many Americans 'running on empty.' There's a lot more talk about energy independence. Some folks are trying renewable sources of energy called biofuels . . ." began CBS's Harry Smith, introducing a June 29, 2006, "Early Show" story about "Bio-town," aka Reynolds, Ind. The town has been held up by the media as an energy-independent utopia. Smith ended the story: "it's happy days out there in Bio-town."

But colorful feature stories about happy days have left audiences ignorant of some crucial facts about the nation's energy supply.

In reality, the United States is actually very self-reliant when it comes to energy. "If we look at total energy—including coal, nuclear and a small but growing share from renewables—the country is over 70% self-sufficient," wrote Daniel

Yergin of Cambridge Energy Research Associates in a January 23 [2007] *Wall Street Journal* commentary.

"The risks do not owe to direct imports from the Middle East, contrary to the widespread belief," Yergin wrote. "Some 81% of oil imports do not come from that region. Thus, only 19% of imports—and 12% of total petroleum consumption—originates in the Middle East." He noted that Canada and Mexico are the two largest sources of U.S. oil imports.

But the primary media focus has remained on hostile nations, especially in the Middle East, excluding those facts.

"What's happening in Iraq has prompted many people across this country to think long and hard about breaking America's dependence on foreign oil. It's not gonna be easy," said ABC's Cynthia McFadden on the Nov. 24, 2006, "Nightline."

Independence Has a Price—for Taxpayers

Support for "energy independence" has actually meant more taxes on oil and could mean even more costly subsidies for alternative energies like ethanol. And rising prices could have the ironic consequence of driving Americans toward cheaper, imported oil.

[In early January 2007] the House Democrats passed a bill that Speaker of the House Nancy Pelosi said would "roll back subsidies on big oil" and invest in alternative energies. And the media agreed, focusing on getting back at Big Oil.

"The package would impose $15 billion in fees, taxes and royalties on oil and gas companies," said CBS's Russ Mitchell on "The Early Show" [on] January 18 [2007]. NBC's Natalie Morales came close to Pelosi's exact words on the January 19 [2007] "Today" show: "The House, meantime, voted to roll back some tax breaks for the oil industry."

But there was much more to the bill, as Myron Ebell of the Competitive Enterprise Institute [CEI] explained.

"The House 100-hour energy legislation is a lose-lose scheme for American consumers and taxpayers. Speaker Pelosi's package would make us more dependent on imports of foreign oil by raising taxes on domestic production," Ebell said in a Jan. 16, 2007 press release.

There is a larger looming question about alternative energy: Is there really a need for energy independence?

American Petroleum Institute's senior tax-policy analyst Mark Kibbe agreed, "If Congress imposes these additional costs on the companies, it just makes them more likely to look overseas." He was quoted by the *Christian Science Monitor* on Jan. 18, 2007.

Media infatuation with ethanol also led to shoddy reporting that left out U.S. ethanol subsidies. "Right now Congress is giving billions to ethanol, biodiesel, and the nuclear industry," Doug Koplow of Earth Track consulting firm said in the same *Christian Science Monitor* article. About $6 billion in 2006 went to subsidize ethanol.

Bush's desire to continue "investing" in ethanol can only mean more mandates and subsidies for the energy source— funded by taxpayers.

"President Bush is proposing a huge expansion of the corporate welfare state," said Ebell, CEI's Director of Energy Policy, in a release dated Jan. 23, 2007.

While Ebell does not believe there is anything wrong with alternative energy, he said, "thirty years of enormous subsidies have not made these technologies competitive in the marketplace."

In addition to market inefficiencies there is a larger looming question about alternative energy: Is there really a need for "energy independence?"

Cato Institute Senior Fellow Jerry Taylor doesn't think so. In fact, he thinks the entire goal is "ludicrous." On May 4,

2005, Taylor and Cato Senior Fellow Peter Van Doren shared that opinion in *National Review*.

"The hostility directed at 'foreign' oil is ridiculous . . . Even if the United States imported *no oil at all* (and if we did not restrict trade), supply disruptions abroad would have a similar effect on our economy as if *all our oil* came from overseas," they explained.

If We Drill It . . .

There are two more ironies in the political and media support for "energy independence." One was outlined by John J. Fialka and David Rogers in the *Wall Street Journal* Jan. 18, 2007.

"There is also a potential disconnect between the goals of Ms. Pelosi's agenda: The increase in domestic oil, gas and coal production likely needed to achieve energy independence would entail heightened output of greenhouse gases," they wrote.

The other irony is that politicians and the media who advocate less dependence on foreign energy sources also oppose drilling for more domestic oil.

"[W]e can do a lot more in this country, you know. The 102 billion barrels of known oil reserves and gas reserves that we don't have access to in this country on federal land and outer continental shelf, we'd like to go produce that," said John Hofmeister, president of Shell Oil, during the June 18, 2006, "Meet the Press" on NBC.

But Democratic politicians such as Speaker of the House Nancy Pelosi are not keen on the prospect of domestic drilling. Following a Senate vote regarding drilling in ANWR [Arctic National Wildlife Refuge] in 2005, Pelosi issued a press release exuding delight. "I am pleased to see our Senate colleagues secured a crucial victory and joined the vast majority of House Democrats to vote for preserving our pristine Arctic National Wildlife Refuge. . . . Republicans have attempted to defile one of our nation's most beautiful areas."

The media have mirrored that view, echoing environmentalists to make ANWR sound heavenly. ABC reporter Bill Weir called it "truly an awe-inspiring place" during the June 12, 2005, "Good Morning America."

Ethanol: Fuel of the Future?

"We must continue investing in new methods of producing ethanol, using everything from wood chips to grasses to agricultural wastes," said President Bush during the 2007 State of the Union address.

Ethanol, an alcohol currently being made from corn that can be used as fuel, has taken center stage and has been promoted by the news media as the panacea that would provide energy independence.

In May 2006, ABC, CBS and NBC all ran positive stories about ethanol and Brazil's success in switching to ethanol derived from sugar cane so that the country would no longer be reliant on oil imports.

"[W]hat if there was one solution to all of this [high gas prices], something that could solve America's energy crisis, strengthen our national security, and help save the planet at the same time?" asked NBC's Stone Phillips during the May 7, 2006, "Dateline."

Phillips left out experts who disagree that ethanol is a planet-saver, but he wouldn't have had to go to conservative think tanks to find them. Daniel Becker of the liberal environmentalist group Sierra Club has said that ethanol is "no boon for the environment."

The expensive process of getting ethanol to the fuel market includes transportation costs.

"It's not a great deal, because you're putting so much energy in to get a modest amount of energy out," Becker said on the April 18, 2006, "CBS Evening News."

Still, journalists have been enamored with Brazil. CBS's Dan Rather stated that "[b]ecause ethanol is cheaper, the law of supply and demand took care of the rest" in Brazil during "60 Minutes" on May 7, 2006.

What Rather was really seeing at work in Brazil was the law of subsidies. "The price at the pump was also subsidized to make the new fuel cheaper than petrol," *BBC News* business reporter Robert Plummer wrote. According to Plummer farmers were also paid "generous subsidies to grow sugar-cane."

The expensive process of getting ethanol to the fuel market includes transportation costs. Ethanol "is made out here on the prairie. It's too corrosive to put in a pipeline, and so 100 percent of it has to be put on a train or a truck or even a barge to get it to market . . . [it] could actually raise gas prices this summer," reporter Wyatt Andrews stated on the April 18, 2006, "CBS Evening News."

Another detail left out by those reports is the amount of fossil fuel that it takes to produce ethanol. According to *Wall Street Journal* columnist John Fund, "Corn farmers have done a good job of disguising the fact that it still takes more than a gallon of fossil fuel—29% more is the best estimate—to make a gallon of ethanol."

Rising demand for ethanol, which is likely to increase if Congress goes along with President Bush's desire to reduce U.S. gasoline usage by 20 percent by 2017, is also driving up the worldwide cost of corn for food and corn syrup–based sweeteners.

The media have also fawned over examples of other energy alternatives. ABC's "Nightline" re-aired a June segment on Nov. 24, 2006, about "Bio-Town," in Reynolds, Ind., "to revisit the story of one small town in the nation's heartland that has decided to try and kick its addiction to oil and become completely energy independent," gushed anchor Cynthia Mc-Fadden.

5

Dependence On Oil Threatens America's Interests

Frederick W. Smith and P.X. Kelley

Frederick W. Smith is chairman, president, and chief executive of FedEx Corp. P.X. Kelley, a retired general, was commandant of the Marine Corp and a member of the Joint Chiefs of Staff under President Ronald Reagan. They are co-chairmen of the Energy Security Leadership Council.

Oil is a fungible global commodity. This means that global supply shortages have global economic impact, and the percentage of foreign versus domestic oil consumed has very little impact on adverse economic impacts of oil shortages. Dependence on oil, regardless of the source, puts America at risk. For economic and national security reasons, U.S. dependence on oil needs to be reduced across the board. Pure market economics will never solve this problem, and thus government leadership is absolutely necessary. Increasing transportation efficiency is the single most effective step the united States can take to improve its oil security.

Could a mere 4 percent shortfall in daily oil supply propel the price of a barrel to more than $120 in a matter of days? That's what some oil market experts are saying, and if they're correct, we face the very real possibility of an oil shock wave that could send our economy reeling. Such a rapid rise in fuel costs would have profound effects that could severely threaten the foundation of America's economic prosperity.

Frederick W. Smith and P.X. Kelley, "Are We Ready for the Next Oil Shock?" *Washington Post*, August 11, 2006, p. A19. Copyright © 2006 The Washington Post Company. Reproduced by permission of the authors.

Global Trends Increase Danger

The global oil trends now at work—rising consumption, reduced spare production capacity and high levels of instability in key oil-producing countries—all increase the likelihood of a supply shock. But unfortunately energy debates in this country often suggest a profound misunderstanding of these international economic dynamics. Calls for "energy independence" notwithstanding, oil is a fungible global commodity, which means that events affecting supply or demand anywhere will affect oil consumers everywhere. A country's exposure to world price shocks is thus a function of the amount of oil it consumes and is not significantly affected by the ratio of domestic to imported petroleum.

> The members of the [Energy Security Leadership] Council are united in the belief that a fundamental shift in energy policy can prevent an unprecedented economic and national security calamity.

The magnitude of our dependence on oil puts stress on our military, strengthens our strategic adversaries and undermines our efforts to support democratic allies. Each year the United States expends enormous military resources protecting the chronically vulnerable oil production and distribution network while also preparing to guarantee international access to key oil-producing regions. This allocation of forces and dollars diminishes the military's capability for dealing with the war on terrorism and other defense priorities.

Considering the potentially devastating impact of an oil crisis, the time has come for new voices, especially those of business leaders and retired national security officials, to join the call for meaningful government action to reduce projected U.S. oil consumption. Our respective personal experiences—running a global transportation and logistics company and spearheading the establishment of an independent U.S. Central Command in the Middle East—convince us that America's extreme dependence on oil is an unacceptable threat to national security and prosperity.

During the coming months, we will be co-chairing the Energy Security Leadership Council, a new and intensive effort by business executives and retired military officers to advance a national energy strategy for reducing U.S. oil dependence. Although drawn from very different backgrounds, the members of the council are united in the belief that a fundamental shift in energy policy can prevent an unprecedented economic and national security calamity.

Looking for Real Change

As President [George W.] Bush and members of Congress construct a strategy for energy security, several central principles should guide them:

The most substantial, rapid and cost-effective gains are almost certain to be achieved by making our transportation system more fuel-efficient. To be sure, the search for increased oil, natural gas and alternative energy supplies merits support, as do strategies for controlling industrial demand. But the transportation sector relies on oil for 97 percent of its energy needs and accounts for 68 percent of total U.S. oil consumption. With the right incentives, America's engineers and businesses could soon provide better vehicle technologies, a more efficient movement of goods and many other smart solutions. Substantially reducing demand in the transportation sector would help ensure availability of affordable supplies for critical industrial, commercial and consumer needs.

Pure market economics will never solve this problem. Markets do not account for the hidden and indirect costs of oil dependence. Businesses focused on the highest return on investment are not always in a position to implement new solutions, many of which depend on technologies and fuels that cannot currently compete with the marginal cost of producing a barrel of oil. Most important of all, the marketplace alone will not act preemptively to mitigate the enormous damage that would be inflicted by a sudden, serious and sustained price increase.

Government leadership is absolutely necessary. Many of the most promising solutions on both the demand and supply sides will require decades to mature. Government proposals should align the interests of businesses and individuals with society's goals; for example, tax credits and similar incentives must allow businesses to recover investments and engage in essential long-range planning, and they must account for the high implicit discount rates that consumers apply to future savings. While recent legislation has pointed us in the right direction, bolder action must be taken.

Whatever the eventual shape of a credible energy security plan, significant public and private resources will be required to put policy into practice. The government needs to do more than just provide funds, though; it must sustain a strategic energy policy even if oil prices drop in the medium term. This is only fitting given the size and nature of the threat. Indeed, if it means condemning the country to another decade of energy dependence, the possible return of $50 oil should be no less frightening than the prospect of an oil shock wave.

6

Dependence On Oil Is Not a Threat to National Security

Shikha Dalmia

Shikha Dalmia is an editorial writer for the Detroit News *and a senior analyst with the Reason Foundation.*

The price of oil is set by the global market. The fates of oil-producing and oil-consuming nations are interdependent, since oil producers depend on purchases of oil to support their economies. International trade in oil fosters peace by motivating hostile trading partners to refrain from acting on their hostility.

As the nuclear stand-off with Iran helped push oil prices to near-record levels, [in 2006] President [George W.] Bush once again declared, "Dependency on oil creates an economic problem for us, and it creates a national security problem for us."

But if Iran's behavior makes the case for anything at all, it is that America should become more—not less—"dependent" on foreign oil. In fact, the best way for America to defuse the so-called Middle Eastern oil weapon is by purchasing even more oil from the region.

The economic case for energy independence has always been nonsensical. It is not possible to shield American consumers from rising prices at the pump simply by replacing foreign oil with domestic oil. Why? Because regardless of where the oil is produced—Oman or Oklahoma—its prices are set by the global market.

Shikha Dalmia, "Defend America, Buy More Iranian Oil: Energy Independence Isn't a Good National Security Strategy," *Reason Online*, May 5, 2006. Reproduced by permission.

The Market for Oil Is Global

The global demand for oil and its ease of transportation have synchronized oil prices everywhere. Therefore, unless compelled by draconian government mandates, no American company that can command $3 a gallon in Oman would sell it for much less in Oklahoma. If war prevents Middle Eastern oil from reaching its global customers, the incentive for American companies to sell U.S. oil overseas would be even greater given the higher prices that it would fetch. War or peace, no amount of domestic production will give us "independence" from the law of supply and demand.

But if domestic production won't ensure access to cheap oil, some believe that it will at least shield us from the kind of geo-political manipulation that Arab countries attempted during the 1973 oil embargo. That, however, is also a myth.

For starters, OPEC [Organization of Petroleum Exporting Countries]—the Arab-dominated cartel of oil producing nations—did not succeed in its manipulation even then. It lifted the embargo in less than two months, once it became clear that while its members were giving up oil revenues, its oil was still reaching the United States because of diverted shipments from Europe. There was some diminution of oil supply in the United States, but not nearly enough to do any serious damage to the American economy.

The long lines outside gas stations that Americans associate with the embargo resulted more from panic buying and domestic oil price controls rather than lost Arab oil, notes M.A. Adelman, a professor of economics at the Massachusetts Institute of Technology.

But if all OPEC countries together couldn't pull off their political blackmail, a rogue regime acting alone will surely not succeed.

Saudi Arabia's experience in 1980 demonstrates why. The country elected to play the role of OPEC's "swing producer," unilaterally limiting its oil production in order to boost world oil prices. It expected that higher oil prices would compensate it for lower oil sales.

But Saudi Arabia was forced to abandon its policy in a few years as other OPEC members bumped up their production on the sly and pushed its exports to nearly zero. Since then, Saudi Arabia has repeatedly said that it would never again unilaterally cut output.

The lesson of Saudi Arabia's experience—oil sales that one producer foregoes will quickly be captured by others—is not lost even on regimes such as Iran, especially now when there are more oil suppliers than ever before.

Given Iran's defiant mood and tension with the U.S. and Europe over its nuclear program, one would have thought that this would be a perfect moment for its hot-headed president to further escalate—if not act on—his threat to cut off Iran's oil exports to the West and shut down oil shipments through the Straits of Hormuz.

Iran Needs to Sell Its Oil

But beneath all of Iran's saber-rattling and its threat to retaliate against Israel in the event of a U.S. attack, it realizes how suicidal such a move would be. During a recent OPEC meeting, Karem Vaziri Hamaneh, Iran's oil minister, went out of his way to reassure the world that Iran had no intention of disrupting the oil market. "The need of the world for energy is soaring and, if Iran is taken out of the equation, prices will shoot up," he told the *Wall Street Journal.* "But we don't want to cause hardship for any consumers around the world."

Vaziri's concern is not so much for the world's oil consumers, of course, as for the economic consequences for his own country. The Iranian government depends on oil exports for nearly half of its total revenues. If it cuts these exports, buyers could go to other suppliers. But there is not much else that Iran could sell to other countries to replace its lost oil revenues.

Our dependence on Middle Eastern oil is only the flip side of their dependence on our purchases. But given the narrow base of Middle Eastern economies, the power in the relationship is firmly on the side of the oil buyers. If that relationship were to end because of "energy independence," we would give up crucial leverage to control the worst behavior of some of the world's worst regimes. Of course, this leverage is no magic wand that would protect us from a totally irrational regime willing to absorb the economic cost of using the oil weapon. But the more oil we get from such a regime, the higher the price it would have to pay.

Thus whatever other arguments there might be for boosting domestic oil production, national security is not one of them. While this might seem counter-intuitive, it is really part of the overall logic of trade: The mutual dependence that trade breeds fosters peace because it gives hostile trading partners an incentive to refrain from acting on their hostility. Energy independence would weaken that incentive.

7

Good Relations with Venezuela Is the Key to U.S. Energy Security

Bernardo Alvarez

Bernardo Alvarez, a former official with the Ministry of Energy and Mines in Venezuela, is Venezuelan ambassador to the United States. He also serves as Venezuelan representative to the Energy Council of the United States.

The United States uses 70 percent of the energy consumed in the Western Hemisphere. Venezuala, with oil reserves equaling 316 billion barrels, holds the largest oil reserves in the world. The United States cannot achieve energy security for itself at the expense of other nations. Rather, it should engage in dialogue with Venezuela and adopt Venezuela's goal of fostering greater integration of the energy needs of the region in order to enhance energy security regionally.

Energy security is one of the major policy issues facing the United States. The debate in this country, however, has been framed solely in terms of whether the United States has adequate supplies of reliable and affordable energy to meet its substantial needs. While certainly a component of energy security in its narrowest sense, it really misstates the issue, making it difficult, if not impossible, for the achievement of real energy security. Unfortunately, the United States is missing the opportunity of gaining a more integrated, robust and durable energy security not only for itself, but also the entire hemisphere, and, more generally, the world as a whole.

In our fast-changing and ever-smaller world, it must be recognized that there needs to be reasonable and affordable availability of energy for all poor and developing countries that otherwise lack adequate energy supplies, the sine qua non for sustainable social and economic development. With economic development comes upward mobility and social stability, both of which are the foundations for true security for all nations, not just a select few. The extreme asymmetries that have for far too long characterized access to energy by rich countries compared to poor countries must be eliminated.

The Enormous Consumption Gap

In the Western Hemisphere, for example, the consumption gap is enormous. The United States, comprising a third of the hemisphere's population, accounts for more than 70 percent of all the energy consumed in the hemisphere. U.S. needs cannot be at the expense of other countries. There really is no choice.

Venezuela also will expand its refining capacity to 4.1 million barrels per day.

In Venezuela, the government of President Hugo Chavez, with its vast oil resources, is addressing this problem. Venezuela is meeting U.S. energy needs, through the supply of crude oil and refined products and through socially-oriented initiatives such as the discounted heating oil program for low-income U.S. families, and helping our own people and other Latin countries. Yet, it is roundly condemned by the U.S. administration for doing so.

It is vitally important to understand the capabilities of Venezuela that permit us to be able to do so. After official certification is completed, which is well under way, Venezuela's official reserves will total 316 billion barrels, making us the holder of the largest oil reserves in the world, surpassing even Saudi Arabia. Our national oil company, Petroleos de Venezuela (PDVSA), will spend a total of $120 billion in capital and operating expenses over the next six years. By 2012, crude oil production in Venezuela will increase to 5.8 million barrels per day. Moreover, sooner than people think, there will only be a handful of countries that will be net exporters of oil, and Venezuela, only four to five days' shipping time from the United States, as opposed to 40 days for oil from the Mideast, will be one of them.

Within the next six years, Venezuela also will expand its worldwide refining capacity to 4.1 million barrels per day. Currently, Venezuela is ultimately responsible for the refining of 3.3 million barrels per day through 24 refineries worldwide, of which six are located in the United States as part of PDVSA's wholly owned U.S. subsidiary, CITGO Petroleum Corp. By 2012, PDVSA will build three new grassroots refineries in Venezuela, one in Brazil in partnership with Petrobras, the Brazilian national oil company, and undertake the expansions of three existing refineries in Uruguay and the Caribbean.

Venezuela Is a Leader

Venezuela's capabilities in energy are far beyond any other country in the hemisphere and rivals those of any country in the world. But Venezuela and PDVSA also realize that the benefits associated with the natural resources of the developing world can no longer flow in only one direction. We are committed to putting our oil revenues to work for all of our people. We are realistically, and systematically, tackling the problems of our country and other Latin American countries, in which economic inequalities have long been the dominant and heartbreaking aspect of society. PDVSA is directly spending billions of dollars to fund sorely needed eduation, medical and poverty-reduction programs throughout Venezuela and Latin America.

Beyond our borders, as part of the effort to eliminate the devastating impact of the asymmetries of energy consumption in our hemisphere, Venezuela has been a leader in creating a program for Caribbean nations, among the poorest in the world, known as Petrocaribe. Through this program, Venezuela is providing these countries affordable oil at market prices through the use of generous financing terms and helping these countries to upgrade their energy supply and distribution infrastructures.

The United States should heed [Venezuela's] call to engage in dialogue ... on the basis of mutual respect between sovereign nations.

Venezuela is also fostering greater integration among all Latin American countries to meet the energy needs of the region. Low-cost oil supplies are being provided to the continent through programs such as Petroandina and Petrosur. In addition, plans have been initiated to construct a 6,200-mile natural gas pipeline from Venezuela all the way to Argentina and to integrate already existing pipelines throughout South America to make the region more self-reliant and environmentally friendly and to permit our countries to work more closely together.

The United States can continue to look only inward in a self-defeating effort to achieve a chimerical "energy security." Or, it can rethink its foreign policy with respect to Latin America. It is a fool's errand for the United States to try to gain "energy independence" for itself. Simply put, it is impossible. Energy independence within the hemisphere can be achieved, however.

Instead of heaping condemnation on us for our vision of what constitutes true energy security for all countries, including the United States, and the means to achieve it, the United States should heed our call to engage in dialogue with us on the basis of mutual respect between sovereign nations.

Venezuela's right to manage its nonrenewable energy resources in ways that provide maximum benefit to its people and the people of the hemisphere, in accordance with the will and dignity of our citizenry, is fundamental. We would welcome the United States' acknowledgement of this right, and we invite it to work with us in a spirit of true comity in this vital endeavor.

8

The United States Should Not Seek to Control Iraqi Oil

Jerry M. Landay

Jerry M. Landay is a writer and former correspondent for CBS News.

A proposed law before the Iraqi Parliament would grant foreign oil companies rights of access to sixty-three Iraqi oil fields, while only seventeen already developed oil fields would be controlled by a proposed Iraqi National Oil Company. The Iraq War is a costly war being waged to gain control of Iraqi oil interests. In an age of terrorism, this kind of policy only makes permanent the threat to American "energy security."

After World War II, the president's national security council propounded a policy that would shape the world's geopolitical future: "Oil operations are, for all practical purposes, instruments of our foreign policy."

More than a half-century later, that policy has not changed.

With the invasion of Iraq already secretly being planned, freshly selected President George W. Bush listed "energy security" as his first action priority.

Energy security is the invisible elephant in Washington, guiding Bush policy on Iraq, the Middle East, Latin America, and Africa. It explains the "surge," the absence of an exit strategy from Iraq, the stubborn resistance of the Bush-Cheney team to efforts by the Congressional Democrats to impose a

Jerry M. Landay, "Jerry Landay: Iraq War is All About Controlling the Oil," The *Providence Journal*, May 11, 2007. Reproduced by permission.

withdrawal deadline for 170,000 American soldiers, as well as the ongoing construction of permanent military bases in Iraq, and the costly stationing of thousands of American troops on foreign soil from Kuwait to Djibouti.

The Explanation for Everything

Energy security is the invisible presence shaping what the 2008 presidential candidates say or don't say about oil and energy. Energy security is the reason [presidential candidate] Hillary Clinton refuses to embrace a withdrawal deadline and why Republican presidential hopeful John McCain declares that there is "no alternative Plan B" to the ongoing build-up of American forces.

In short, the American occupation and the maintenance of a shaky Iraqi government are the insurance policy for American control and access to the second largest untapped reserve of petroleum in the world. The politicians don't say much about an energy-security policy based on foreign oil. The news media don't report very much on it.

The Big Five oil companies don't proclaim it in their self-promoting institutional advertising campaigns. Yet the so-called "Majors"—U.S.-based Exxon-Mobil, Chevron, and ConocoPhillips; the Dutch Shell Oil; and the British-owned British Petroleum—would be the principal beneficiaries of a new hydrocarbon law before the Iraqi Parliament that the press rarely mentions.

The initial draft, shaped by American contractors to the Iraqi government, has been amended by the U.S. Embassy in Iraq, and approved by the Iraqi Cabinet. The draft now awaits final approval by the Iraqi Parliament, but there is much reported Iraqi resistance to it, with good reason.

Oil Change International an energy watchdog group, has devotedly tracked the proposed law. The law would reverse a trend in which most major petro-nations have largely nationalized their oil fields and reserves. Under the proposed Iraqi law, concessions involving 63 Iraqi oilfields, both developed and undeveloped, would go to major foreign-oil companies, assuring them of dominance over Iraqi oil for a generation or more. Only 17 already developed fields would be directly controlled by a proposed Iraqi National Oil Company (INOC).

What the Law Will Do

One of the key provisions of the draft law states that "the overall allocation of exploration and production rights . . . shall aim at achieving variety among oil companies and operators . . . so as to enhance efficiency through positive competition."

The draft law grants assurance of "reasonable incentives" to foreign investors—the provision that kicks the door open to foreign developers. Development licenses are to be granted "on a competitive basis," a nod to outside companies with sufficient development capital.

Oil Change International states: "The law is a dramatic break from the past. Foreign oil companies will have a stake in Iraq's vast oil wealth for the first time since 1972, when Iraq nationalized the oil industry. This law would essentially open two-thirds of known—and all of [Iraq's] as yet undiscovered—reserves to foreign control." According to Oil Change International, this amounts to 115 billion barrels of known oil reserves—10 percent of the world total.

The language of Article 11 of the draft law pays vague lip service to the principle of equal revenue sharing from petroleum and natural gas proceeds among Shi'as, Sunnis, and Kurds—supporting "distribution of . . . revenues monitoring of federal revenue allocation." But ConocoPhillips and Shell are already negotiating separate concessions with Kurdistan alone, and others reportedly will follow suit.

Oil Change International reports that foreign oil companies "would not have to invest their earnings in the Iraqi economy, partner with Iraqi companies, hire Iraqi workers or share new technologies. They could even ride out Iraq's current instability by signing contracts now, while the Iraqi government is at its weakest, and then wait at least two years before setting foot in the country."

Washington politicians understandably want to hedge the nation against the devastating impact on American life and the economy of a severe interruption of overseas oil supplies. But waging costly resource wars or granting discriminatory privileges to private interests that harm host oil states in an age of terrorism only makes permanent the threat to American "energy security."

Only "soft power"—peacemaking, smart diplomacy, constructive nation-building, generous sharing formulas, vigorous energy conservation and research policies at home—can assure long-term security for American interests without creating grievous new problems. It's time for leadership from politicians to acknowledge the existence of the elephant in the room and do something creative about it.

9

The United States Should Be More Involved in Iraqi Oil Development

Michael Makovsky

From 2002 to 2006, Michael Makovsky was a special assistant for Iraqi oil policy in the office of the secretary of defense.

Although Iraqi oil revenues have grown almost 30 percent each year since 2004, this is mostly due to increases in the price of oil. Production levels have been stagnant. This is not just the result of poor security. The Iraqi government has made little progress in producing legislation on issues such as foreign investment, taxation, and contracting, which is necessary to stabilize the Iraqi oil industry. The United States should provide targeted guidance in these and other critical areas so that Iraq can generate greater revenues from its oil resources.

On March 27, 2003, Paul Wolfowitz, then deputy secretary of defense, predicted that Iraq's oil revenue would "finance" its reconstruction and do so "relatively soon." With wise investment and management, Wolfowitz might have been right. Even though its oil sector accounts for 95 percent of the Iraqi state's revenue and is essential to the country's ability to one day pay its own way, the United States has yet to make a serious effort to boost the Iraqi oil industry, which controls the second or third largest reserves (mostly undeveloped) in the world. President George W. Bush's recent Iraq plan is no better in this regard.

Revenues Have Grown but Production Has Not

Despite Iraq's violence and political difficulties, its oil revenue has grown about 30 percent each year since 2004, topping $30 billion in 2006. This achievement, however, was due mostly to high oil prices, which, as the recent broad price drop indicates, cannot be counted on in the future. According to State Department figures, production has been stagnant at 2.1 million barrels per day, or 400,000 barrels per day below the immediate prewar peak (which was matched for a few months in 2004). The shortfall from even this modest target represents a loss of over $7 billion annually (based on $50 per barrel of Iraqi oil) and about 15 percent of unused, or spare, global oil production capacity (a significant amount in a still tight market).

Many in and out of government accept the conventional wisdom that security problems are to blame. Indeed, security problems have contributed to smuggling and irregular oil exporting through the north to Turkey, as well as limited refining and uneven distribution of gasoline and other petroleum products. And certainly if violence were to spread to the southern oil facilities, Iraq could suffer a longstanding loss of significant oil production and exports.

But putting all the blame on security is mistaken. To illustrate this error simply, there have been few attacks in the south, where over 80 percent of Iraqi oil is produced, and yet oil production and exports there have been generally stagnant for over three years.

Blaming the lack of security masks the serious problem of poor Iraqi and U.S. management of vital oil projects.

Blaming the lack of security masks the serious problem of poor Iraqi and U.S. management of vital oil projects. Most notably, Iraq's overwhelmed and centralized bureaucracy, increasingly fearful of accusations of corruption, has managed to spend only a fraction of the Iraqi funds available for oil projects in the past couple of years. Through underinvestment, the United States also hobbled initial efforts to improve Iraq's oil revenue, despite the potential for even small upgrades in Iraq's oil sector to result in spectacular financial returns for the Iraqis. Fears that a more assertive policy would fuel conspiracy theories and upset Iraq's oil-exporting neighbors (who are supposedly worried that a resurgence of Iraqi oil production would oversupply the market and reduce their market share) has led Washington to seek only to restore facilities to their prewar condition. In contrast, after many years of watching their country's oil capacity decline because of war, sanctions, and looting, several senior Iraqi oil officials sought to boost oil production and exports. Too bad this point of view was not more widely shared. Some U.S. and Coalition Provisional Authority officials have seemed to believe the oil industry does not need much funding at all. And what little funding has been allocated has been interrupted by delays and contracting procedures, when not mismanaged or spent to import fuel. The result has been a practice of underinvestment in a sector that should be yielding enormous financial returns.

The past notwithstanding, the [George W.] Bush administration should bring greater focus to this issue. The White House views oil primarily as a political vehicle to unite Iraqis instead of as a means to advance Iraq's economy and self-sufficiency. In his January 10 [2007] address, Bush limited discussion of oil to the question of equitable revenue-sharing and Iraq's need for a good law to bring that about. Perhaps such a law will contribute to national political reconciliation, but the issues involved are very complex, and agreement and implementation could take far longer than the media and perhaps even the White House imagine.

One Law Is Not Enough

There needs to be, however, not one oil law but a multilaw hydrocarbon regime to address not only revenue-sharing but also foreign investment, taxation, contracting, the establishment of a decision-making federal petroleum committee, and the reestablishment of Iraqi national oil companies, among other vital matters. Revenue-sharing might be part of the horse-trading, but its resolution should not be a precondition for addressing every other issue. For any such agreements to become law under Iraq's constitution, a draft law must pass through the Council of Ministers and then Parliament. If any constitutional amendments are required to accommodate any new oil laws, the process will go on even longer.

While this whole process plays out, the Iraqi oil sector will continue to deteriorate, to the short- and long-term detriment of Iraq's ability to become self-sufficient. Iraqi oil stagnation or decline will also contribute a bullish element to the global oil market, which is certainly not constructive to U.S. economic or strategic interests.

Thus, the U.S. government should be looking beyond the politics of Iraqi oil to help Iraq pursue the economic advantages of developing its oil sector. Here are some practical ways the United States can help.

First, Washington should work to bolster necessary Iraqi and U.S. technical expertise in Baghdad. The number of excellent Iraqi oil officials, many of whom trained abroad, is quickly dwindling because of age, security, and ministry politicization. The United States needs to encourage the Ministry of Oil to hire outside experts in contracting, project management, security, and other important areas, and integrate them into its bureaucracy just as Russian, Saudi, and other national oil companies have hired foreign experts. Likewise, the U.S. State Department must rely less on diplomats and more on private sector experts to run and reform its reconstruction operations. Broadly, [the Department of] State should withdraw generalist civilian ministerial advisers in favor of targeted industry experts, to whom the Iraqis will be more likely to listen.

> *The United States should provide targeted guidance and assistance, so that Iraq can generate greater revenue in the near and long term.*

Second, Washington should hike its funding for training Iraqi oil officials beyond the current $2.5 million managed by the Trade and Development Agency, and conduct extensive training in the United States as some senior Iraqi oil officials have requested. Most training is conducted elsewhere in the Mideast because of cost and U.S. visa difficulties. But it would better serve U.S. interests to train future Iraqi oil leaders here, where they can improve their English, study our ways, and develop relationships with a range of U.S. oil executives and government officials. Russia, Britain, China, and others have hosted hundreds of Iraqi oil officials for extended training in their home countries.

Third, the United States should facilitate the expenditure of additional funds to increase Iraqi oil production, export, and storage capacity, particularly in the south. Some projects, such as oil well refurbishments, can quickly bring superb returns. Of course, the Iraqis must spend some of their own money, but the United States must not wait for that to happen. Whatever the Iraqis do not spend now, they will certainly need later anyway.

Fourth, the United States ought to dedicate more resources to infrastructure security in the south, which suffers fewer attacks than the center or north but is far more important to the oil industry. While the United States can help with money and personnel, Iraq must take overall responsibility for infrastructure security and bring in private contractors to help with training and guarding key facilities—the cost of which will be offset by the extra oil revenue generated.

The Iraqis must take the lead in developing and securing their highly promising oil industry. But the United States should provide targeted guidance and assistance, so that Iraq can generate greater revenue in the near and long term. That remains an essential condition for reviving and stabilizing Iraq and finally reducing its dependency on the U.S. military and taxpayer.

10

Coal Is the Key to America's Energy Future

Craig Thomas

Craig Thomas is a Republican U.S. senator from Wyoming and a member of the Energy and Natural Resources Committee.

Coal is the United States's largest domestic energy reserve and can play an important role in the development of a self-reliant strategy for national energy security.

If you have filled up your car with gas recently, you have probably noticed that your wallet might be lighter than usual. In [May 2007], the average price for gasoline rose to an all-time high, breaking $3 for a gallon of gas. In fact, some experts are predicting that gas prices could possibly reach $4 a gallon in the near future. These rising gas prices are placing an undue burden squarely on the backs of every American.

Increased gas prices are [usually] explained as a simple case of inefficient supply and increasing demand. We are continuing to face a lack of production capacity and unexpected outages at our oil refineries while our robust economy is moving ahead consuming more energy. We, of course, must evaluate ways to moderate our consumption, but given recent efforts in the Senate, I would like to focus for now on factors restricting the supply.

Lack of Refinery Capacity

Because of high costs, cumbersome regulations and opposition to new refinery construction, our country has not built any new facilities since 1976. A series of recent outages at one

Craig Thomas, "Guest Opinion: Coal Key to America's Energy Future," *Billings Gazette*, May 16, 2007. Reproduced by permission of the estate of Craig Thomas.

of our largest refineries have resulted in major reductions in available domestic gasoline. The lack of domestic refining capacity also increases our reliance on foreign sources of refined gasoline. The volatility of the regions of the world where we import more than 60 percent of our transportation fuels has created upward pressure on the price that consumers face at the pump. America now imports about a million barrels of gasoline every day—that means that about one of every 10 gallons of gas Americans get at the pump is refined in a foreign country. Fortunately, there is a common-sense solution to this problem.

We can begin to ensure our energy security by developing major energy sources right here at home, using advanced fuel technology to produce new, clean-burning products like coal-derived fuels. Taking advantage of coal, our largest domestic energy reserve, we can provide a readily available and flexible fuel source for our country now that can continue to be used in the future.

Our focus now is to have a responsive national energy policy that builds upon the significant achievements of the 2005 Energy Policy Act. I believe security, affordability and environmental impact are the most important issues to address. Coal has a significant role to play in this context, and it is fully capable of fulfilling our need to address all three categories.

Better Than Ethanol

In a recent Senate Energy Committee meeting, I introduced an amendment to advance the use of coal as a fuel source. My amendment is designed to improve our nation's fuel supply by making 21 billion gallons of coal-derived fuel available over the next 15 years. The evidence in support of coal is overwhelming—there's no question that coal must continue to be a major part of our nation's energy needs, especially in providing ultra clean diesel for businesses and consumers as well as jet fuel for our military aircraft.

Unfortunately, Senate Democrats on the committee locked arms and defeated the amendment because they believe it threatens their goal for a massive increase in the production of ethanol—more than four times the current federally mandated amount. Although ethanol provides advantages as a fuel additive, it is no substitute for gasoline or diesel and it presents some other potential serious problems:

- First, the production of ethanol has already begun to increase the price of livestock feed and food.

- Second, it doesn't have the necessary infrastructure in place to get it to market. Ethanol has to be delivered using the same trucks and railroads that rely on diesel to deliver this additive to market.

- Third, its environmental benefits are not proving to be nearly as significant as proponents originally claimed and maintain.

As I mentioned, it is important for us to remember that ethanol is an additive; it is not a stand-alone fuel that we can put in our cars and trucks. However, coal-derived fuel is a sole-source fuel and can be developed for use in today's vehicles—we are moving ahead with plans for the construction of a coal-to-liquids plant in Carbon County [Wyoming] to produce clean diesel.

Members of Congress must begin to realize the opportunities we have with our nation's largest fossil fuel resource. The quicker we capitalize on this large resource and move forward to make coal more clean and efficient, the faster we'll have an answer to our nation's energy needs.

11

Coal-Based Energy Independence Threatens the Environment

Bradford Plumer

Bradford Plumer writes for the New Republic, *a weekly current affairs magazine.*

Recently the coal industry has joined the "energy security" craze to begin promoting liquefied coal as the solution to the nation's energy problems. Democrats, who in the past have preferred to talk about reducing dependence on foreign oil rather than addressing global warming directly, have joined Republicans in supporting measures aimed at increasing the use of liquefied coal; however, carbon emissions from coal equal or exceed those from oil. The drive for energy independence could become a threat to the environment because Democrats have chosen to embrace the idea of energy security rather than confront the problem of global warming directly.

In January of 2007, when [Speaker of the House] Nancy Pelosi formed a House committee to focus on climate change, she dubbed it the Select Committee on Energy Independence and Global Warming. The phrasing itself was noteworthy. When environmentalists talk about energy policy, they usually focus, loudly and clearly, on global warming. Many Democrats, however, prefer to frame the discussion in terms of "energy security." And who can blame them? Even people

Bradford Plumer, "Mine, Mine, Mine," The *New Republic*, May 29, 2007. Reproduced by permission of the *New Republic*.

who shrug at the thought of rising temperatures agree that the country should wean itself off foreign oil. It's a hugely popular idea. And, since many of the policies that would free the United States from the clutches of OPEC [Organization of Petroleum Exporting Countries] would *also* curb carbon emissions, who would begrudge the Democrats this bit of clever framing?

But the strategy comes with a downside: The coal industry has lately latched on to the "energy security" craze by billing itself as the answer to our oil-dependency woes. Specifically, Big Coal is teaming up with an array of Republicans and Democrats to tout liquefied coal as a substitute for gasoline in U.S. vehicles. The country is sitting on vast coal reserves, they reason, so why not use those instead of tossing money at the House of Saud? There's just one catch: Liquefied coal would do little to reduce carbon emissions and, in all likelihood, would make things worse. Nevertheless, the idea continues to gain currency in Congress, in part because "energy security" is a sales pitch few politicians can resist.

Not a New Idea

The idea of using coal as a liquid fuel has been around ever since two German scientists in the 1920s discovered the process used to create it. Liquefied coal powered the Nazi military during World War II, and, in the '70s, [President] Jimmy Carter asked Congress to look into coal-to-liquid plants as a way to counter high oil prices. (Six years and billions of dollars in subsidies later, the program was finally killed.) Recently, the Pentagon has revived the idea in a big way, with the Air Force looking to have its entire fleet capable of running on liquefied coal by 2010. No one, after all, worries more about energy security than the U.S. military, among the biggest gas-guzzling entities on the planet.

Enter the coal industry, which has fallen on hard times. Environmentalists managed to halt the construction of eight new coal plants in Texas [in early 2007], while both [former vice president and noted environmentalist] Al Gore and NASA's [National Aeronautics and Space Administration's] James Hansen have called for a moratorium on "dirty" coal plants. Moreover, according to one MIT [Massachusetts Institute of Technology] analysis, if Congress passes a strong emissions-reduction bill to deal with climate change, coal production could decline sharply in the coming years. As a result, investors have been increasingly wary of financing new coal-related projects.

Liquefied coal could be just the life raft Big Coal needs. In late March—to great fanfare on Capitol Hill—the industry unveiled the Coal-to-Liquids Coalition, which will push for federal subsidies for the construction of liquid-coal plants (dozens are being planned) as well as mandates for the fuel itself. The coalition's members include the National Mining Association, the United Mineworkers of America, and the AFL-CIO's [American Federation of Labor-Congress of Industrial Organizations's] Industrial Union Council—groups that carry a great deal of influence on both sides of the aisle [in Congress].

Double the Carbon Emissions

Unfortunately for them, a recent analysis by the Energy Department found that coal-to-liquid fuel could generate roughly twice the carbon emissions that regular gasoline does. Coal backers counter that, if the carbon released during liquefication could be captured and permanently stored underground, the fuel would be comparable in carbon impact to gasoline—that is, the status quo. But the technology for storing carbon underground remains unproved, and, even if it works, cost pressures may prevent it from being adopted on a large scale, since it could make plants more expensive to build and operate. No wonder, then, that recent coal-to-liquid proposals in

Congress merely say that plants need to be *capable* of carbon capture rather than requiring it.

Yet, despite these problems with liquid coal, Democrats are hopping aboard. Nick Rahall, a West Virginian who heads the House Natural Resources Committee, is a major proponent of liquefied coal, calling it the key to energy independence. Another big Democratic supporter is Virginia's Rick Boucher, who chairs the energy subcommittee that will help craft global-warming legislation. (In March [2007], the day before Gore spoke on Capitol Hill, the coal industry held a $1,000-a-head fund-raiser for Boucher.) In the Senate, Barack Obama has co-sponsored the Coal-to-Liquid Fuel Promotion Act of 2007. Playing on the much-beloved energy-security theme, Obama has noted that liquefied coal is "crucial . . . to reduce our dependence on foreign oil." To his credit, Obama has insisted that he will only support the technology if it doesn't lead to an increase in carbon emissions, and he has pushed a rule that could make "dirty" liquid-coal plants unfeasible down the road. But that initiative is unlikely to pass any time soon. "This might be too far ahead of the Senate," says one staffer.

The Coal-to-Liquids Coalition insists that liquid coal is 'among the most practical, promising answers to greater energy security.'

For their part, Republicans seem to have few qualms about coal. In a little-noticed shift, President [George W.] Bush has started talking about mandates for "alternative" as well as "renewable" fuel to replace gasoline—a sign that he's willing to back liquefied coal. Meanwhile, Republicans on the Senate Energy and Natural Resources Committee recently tried to amend an energy package to require that 21 billion gallons of coal-based fuel be used annually by 2022, and, while the gambit was temporarily beaten back, they may still get their way once the bill goes to the Senate floor.

Not a Cheap Solution

Ironically, for all the hype, liquefied coal is hardly the cheapest or easiest way to achieve energy security. According to the National Coal Council, an advisory board to the Department of Energy filled with coal executives, a tremendous coal-to-liquid push—involving $211 billion in investments over the next 20 years and a 40 percent increase in mining—would allow the United States to replace just 10 percent of its oil supply. By contrast, using that coal to generate electricity for plug-in hybrids would displace twice the oil and emit a fraction of the carbon.

Still, the Coal-to-Liquids Coalition insists that liquid coal is "among the most practical, promising answers to greater energy security." And, so long as official Washington continues to treat this dubious assertion as fact, Democrats who prefer to talk about energy independence first and global warming second will be playing right into Big Coal's hands.

12

Using Home-Grown Ethanol Can Contribute to Energy Independence

Joel Makower

Joel Makower is a cofounder of Clean Edge, Inc., a research and publishing firm that focuses on building markets for clean-energy technologies.

General Motors, the State of California, Chevron, and Pacific Ethanol have formed a partnership to demonstrate the feasibility of E-85, a corn-based ethanol and gasoline mix, as an environmentally friendly motor vehicle fuel. The manufacture of flex-fuel vehicles, which can run on conventional gasoline or plant-based ethanol, could lead to a significant reduction in the use of imported oil.

At the 2006 L.A. [Los Angeles] Auto Show, General Motors [GM] took a small but important step toward the goal of fuel diversification and energy independence. It wasn't the debut of a slick concept car or a hybrid or fuel-cell-powered vehicle—the grist of most modern auto shows. Rather, it was an initiative to provide new fueling opportunities for the millions of vehicles already on the road that can run seamlessly on either conventional gasoline or plant-based ethanol.

These so-called flex-fuel vehicles, or FFVs, represent a largely ignored solution to reducing America's oil dependency, and GM has made them a cornerstone of its environmental

Joel Makower, "General Motors and the Road to Energy Independence," WorldChanging.com, January 8, 2006. Reproduced by permission.

strategy. (Full disclosure: GreenOrder, the consultancy with which I am affiliated, has provided strategic counsel to GM on its FFV initiatives.) In its most recent announcement, GM said it would lead a joint demonstration project along with the state of California, Chevron Technology Ventures, and Pacific Ethanol "to learn more about consumer awareness and acceptance of E85 as a motor vehicle fuel by demonstrating its use in GM's flexible-fuel vehicles."

GM currently has 1.5 million vehicles on U.S. roads capable of using a blend of gasoline that contains up to 85% ethanol (referred to as E85), which is mostly derived from corn. (Its principal U.S. competitor, Ford, also has a significant number of FFVs on the road.) E85 vehicles can run on either conventional gas or E85 without any additional modifications, aftermarket conversions, or cumbersome switches for vehicle users. The cars automatically sense the current fuel mix and adjust accordingly.

An Opportunity to Lead

Why push FFVs and E85? GM has several strategic reasons. First and foremost, the company has been under tremendous pressure from environmental groups and others to improve the fuel-efficiency of its vehicles. GM has been slow to market with hybrids, having invested untold millions in next-gen hydrogen fuel cell technology. GM views that strategy as forward-thinking, though many of its critics see it as a dodge to avoid improving the fuel efficiency of its current crop of cars and trucks.

So, FFVs offer a way for GM to demonstrate its environmental leadership and generate sales—and to help jump-start a much-needed flexible-fuel infrastructure along the way.

Just as with hydrogen-powered vehicles, simply putting FFVs on the road isn't enough. You've got to have in place the filling stations that allow motorists to fuel up on E85 and other alternative fuels. And you've got to have an adequate and cost-competitive supply of the fuels themselves. Therein lies the chicken-and-egg dilemma that's led some researchers to predict that a robust hydrogen infrastructure—and, thus, a robust fuel-cell vehicle marketplace—could be as much as two decades off.

Brazil has shown that an ethanol infrastructure is both possible and profitable.

But that's not the case with E85, which is available today, at least in a few outlets. The number of E85 stations in the U.S. doubled [in 2005] to about 600 and is expected to continue to grow as the new Energy Security Act of 2005 is implemented. That law provides a lucrative federal tax credit to stations that install E85 fueling tanks. But even a tenfold increase in ethanol availability would be a drop in the bucket compared to the nation's 176,000 gas stations.

Infrastructure Must Be Built

GM's recent announcement is designed to help grow that infrastructure. Under its partnership, GM flex-fuel vehicles will be used by the California Department of Transportation (CalTrans) at various operations in the state. Chevron Technology Ventures will work with CalTrans to provide E85 fuel and install the necessary refueling pumps in these locations. Pacific Ethanol, a California-based ethanol production and marketing company, will provide the ethanol to Chevron Technology Ventures for the project. All told, it's the kind of systemic, cooperative approach we need to see more of.

Brazil already has shown that an ethanol infrastructure is both possible and profitable. Today, half of all new cars sold there are FFVs, and that will rise to 100% within four years. Brazil's reliance on oil imports has plummeted from 85 percent of its energy consumption in 1978 to nearly zero, Brazilian officials say. Brazil's sugar and ethanol factories not only produce fuel for cars, they generate their own thermal and electric energy using bagasse (the residue of sugar cane crushing) as a fuel in co-generation systems, selling excess electricity to the public grid. Largely as a result of such savvy infrastructure investments, the country is becoming a net exporter of ethanol made from sugar cane, and is "scrambling to invest in port infrastructure to keep ahead of expected growth in world demand for the biofuel," according to Reuters [newswire].

Infrastrucutre issues aside, E85 is far from perfect and, like practically everything else, has trade-offs. For example, E85 holds less energy per gallon than gasoline, reducing one's fuel economy slightly. But E85 ethanol has higher octane, providing increased horsepower, thereby improving vehicle performance somewhat. E85 use also reduces tailpipe emissions of greenhouse gases and some smog-forming exhaust. It's usually price-competitive with conventional gas.

Tweaking the Energy Equation

Beyond that is the issue of corn, the source of nearly all ethanol in the U.S. Modern corn farming is energy and chemical intensive. Early ethanol plants were also energy intensive, raising concerns as to whether the transportation fuel being produced was worth the energy going into making it. Ethanol production currently consumes about 11% of the total U.S. corn crop.

But producing today's ethanol is more efficient. According to the U.S. Energy Department:

> The most official study of the issue, which also reviews other studies, concludes that the "net energy balance" of making fuel ethanol from corn grain is 1.34; that is, for every unit of energy that goes into growing corn and turning it into ethanol, we get back about one-third more energy as automotive fuel. That may not sound impressive, but bear in mind that while the gasoline that ethanol displaces is

largely imported and a high-level pollution source, the mix of energy inputs for producing bioethanol includes much domestic and relatively cleaner energy.

Still, there are better, more energy- and environmentally friendly ways to make ethanol. Energy Department studies show that producing ethanol from some types of plants or crop waste—known as "cellulosic ethanol"—instead of from corn or other crops has an impressive net energy ratio of more than 5:1. It's at that level that E85 becomes a true environmentally friendly fuel. Researchers are making strides in bringing affordable cellulosic ethanol to market.

There's clearly an E85-powered bandwagon taking shape. In his state-of-the-state address [in January 2006], New York Gov. George Pataki promoted a plan to "provide for the establishment of refineries that make ethanol out of agricultural products from our farms and wood products from our northern forests" and to make such fuel "tax-free throughout the entire state."

But one step at a time. For now, GM seems to be moving the needle on flexible fuels, slowly but surely helping to grow the amount of non-petroleum, American-grown energy we put in our tanks. FFVs aren't a substitute for highly efficient vehicles, of course, but they represent an important strategy for GM to burnish its environmental credentials and build markets for greener vehicles—and to create benefits for American farmers and drivers, too.

13

Ethanol Will Not Contribute to U.S. Energy Independence

Robert Bryce

Robert Bryce is managing editor of Energy Tribune *magazine.*

The political establishment has come out strongly in favor of ethanol production as a way to U.S. energy independence; however, many problems undermine the rosy scenario that has been painted for ethanol. Ethanol would require massive government subsidies yet would not be able to replace a significant amount of oil; it would damage air quality and cause the prices of food to rise. Embracing ethanol as an energy independence solution is irrational and is motivated by politics rather than by scientific facts.

Ethanol is a magic elixir. It allows politicians and political operatives to promise voters that America can achieve "energy independence." In this new energy Valhalla, American farmers will be rich, fat and happy, thanks to all the money they will be making from "energy crops." Better yet, U.S. soldiers will never again need to visit the Persian Gulf—except, perhaps, on vacation. With enough ethanol-blended motor fuel, America can finally dictate terms to those rascally Arab sheikhs with their rag-covered heads, multiple wives and supertankers loaded with sulfurous crude.

George W. Bush believes. In January [2007], he declared that the U.S. should be producing 35 billion gallons of etha-

Robert Bryce, "Despite Its Huge Flaws, Ethanol Is Political Holy Water in DC," The *Washington Spectator*, July 7, 2007. Copyright © 2007 Independent Media Institute. All rights reserved. Reproduced by permission of the author.

nol and other alternative fuels by 2017. During a March [2007] trip to Latin America, where he signed an agreement to expand ethanol-related trade between the U.S. and Brazil, Bush said that he was "very upbeat about the potential of biofuel and ethanol."

Not to be outdone, former North Carolina senator John Edwards declared that the U.S. should be producing 65 billion gallons of ethanol per year by 2025. He claims that his proposed New Economy Energy Fund will "develop new methods of producing and using ethanol, including cellulosic ethanol, and offer loan guarantees to new refineries."

Even longtime ethanol foe Senator John McCain—who in the past has called ethanol "highway robbery" and a "giveaway to special interests"—has become an ethanol evangelist. [In] August [2006], during a visit to Iowa, the Republican presidential hopeful called ethanol "a vital alternative energy source not only because of our dependency on foreign oil but its greenhouse-gas reduction effects."

Every major presidential candidate has come out in favor of ethanol. So have the Democrats on Capitol Hill. Speaker of the House Nancy Pelosi wants automakers to build more ethanol-fueled vehicles and wants to see "America's farmers fueling America's energy independence."

It all sounds wonderful. But there are a bushelful of problems with ethanol, none of which fit neatly into a politician's soundbite. Of those many problems, four stand out: the massive subsidies; ethanol's inability to displace significant amounts of imported oil; its deleterious effect on air quality; and its effect on food prices.

Inconvenient Facts

First, the subsidies. Making ethanol from corn borders on fiscal insanity. It uses taxpayer money to make subsidized motor fuel from the single most subsidized crop in America. Between 1995 and 2005, federal corn subsidies totaled $51.2 billion. In 2005 alone, according to data compiled by the Environmental Working Group, corn subsidies totaled $9.4 billion. That $9.4 billion is approximately equal to the budget for the U.S. Department of Commerce, a federal agency that has 39,000 employees.

Need another comparison? That $9.4 billion is nearly twice as much as the federal government spends on WIC, short for the Special Supplemental Nutrition Program for Women, Infants and Children, a program that provides health care and nutrition assistance for low-income mothers and children under the age of five.

Corn subsidies dwarf all other agricultural subsidy programs. The $51.2 billion that American taxpayers spent on corn subsidies between 1995 and 2005 was twice as much as the amount spent on wheat subsidies, more than twice as much as the amount spent on cotton, four times as much as the amount spent on soybeans and 96 times as much as the total subsidies for tobacco during that period.

No matter how you slice it, ethanol production is just too small to have a significant effect on the overall energy market in the U.S.

But the ethanol lobby isn't satisfied with the subsidies paid out to grow the grain. They are also getting huge subsidies to turn that grain into fuel. According to the Global Subsidies Initiative, meeting Bush's goal of producing 35 billion gallons of renewable and alternative fuels per year by 2017 will require total subsidies of $118 billion. The group claims that the $118 billion price tag "would be the minimum subsidy" over the eleven-year period. In a report released on February 9, [2007,] the group said that adding in tax breaks that the corn distillers are getting from state and local governments and federal tariffs imposed on foreign ethanol (mostly from Brazil) "would likely add tens of billions of dollars of subsidies" to the $118 billion estimate.

Despite the subsidies, ethanol has always been more expensive than gasoline. Between 1982 and 2006, the price of ethanol never dropped below that of gasoline—even though ethanol contains just two-thirds of the heat energy of gasoline. That lower energy content means a car using ethanol gets worse gas mileage than one that uses gasoline.

Not Enough Fuel to Make a Difference

The second problem: no matter how you slice it, ethanol production is just too small to have a significant effect on the overall energy market in the U.S.

Ethanol advocates talk about how domestically produced alcohol will reduce the amount of oil America imports. But by any measure, the total energy produced by America's ethanol plants borders on the insignificant. In 2006, the U.S. produced about 5 billion gallons of ethanol. That's the equivalent of just 215,264 barrels of oil per day. For comparison, the U.S. now consumes over 21 million barrels of oil per day. Thus, ethanol provides just one percent of total U.S. oil consumption.

Ethanol will never make a big dent in America's oil imports. And that's true even if all the corn grown in America were turned into ethanol. The U.S. Department of Agriculture estimates that distillers can get 2.7 gallons of ethanol out of one bushel of corn. In 2006, U.S. farmers produced about 10.5 billion bushels of corn.

Converting all that corn into fuel would produce about 28.3 billion gallons of ethanol. However, ethanol's lower heat content means that the actual output would be equivalent to 18.7 billion gallons of gasoline, or about 1.2 million barrels per day. (The U.S. currently imports 10.1 million barrels per day.) Even if the U.S. turned all its corn crop into ethanol, it would supply less than 6 percent of America's total oil needs.

What about cellulosic ethanol, the fuel that can be made from grass, wood, and straw? Al Gore claims that cellulosic ethanol will be "a huge new source of energy, particularly for the transportation sector. You're going to see it all over the place." Bill Clinton says there's enough biomass to "make cellulosic ethanol all over America." Bush, in his 2006 State of the Union speech, said that he wanted to make cellulosic ethanol "practical and competitive within six years."

Alas, cellulosic ethanol is like the tooth fairy, an entity that many people believe in, but no one ever sees. Despite years of hype, there is no significant production of cellulosic ethanol, except in very small, non-commercial distilleries. Maybe that's a good thing, because the more ethanol that's burned in American automobiles, the worse the air quality gets—a fact that leads to the third problem.

The Environmental Protection Agency's [EPA's] website says the agency's mission is "to protect human health and the environment." And yet when it comes to ethanol, the EPA has stated in very clear language that increased use of ethanol in gasoline will mean worse air quality in America.

Of course, that's not the official story. In an April 10 [2007] press release announcing the Renewable Fuel Standard—the federal program mandated by Congress when it passed the Energy Policy Act of 2005—EPA Administrator Stephen L. Johnson declared that the use of more ethanol "offers the American people a hat trick—it protects the environment, strengthens our energy security, and supports America's farmers."

The negative health effects of ethanol-blended gasoline have placed the EPA in the odd position of enforcing rules that run directly counter to its stated goals.

Yet on that very same day, Johnson's agency issued a fact sheet that said using more ethanol will result in major increases in the release of two of the worst air pollutants: volatile organic compounds and nitrogen oxides. The fact sheet said that "Nationwide, EPA estimates an increase in total emissions of volatile organic compounds and nitrogen oxides (VOC + NO$_x$) [of] between 41,000 and 83,000 tons." It went on, saying, "areas that experience a substantial increase in ethanol may see an increase in VOC emissions between four and five percent and an increase in NO$_x$ emissions between 6 and 7 percent from gasoline powered vehicles and equipment."

Serious Air Quality Issues

NO$_x$ is a precursor to fine particulate, which is known to cause thousands of premature deaths each year. VOCs lead to the creation of ground-level ozone, one of the most dangerous urban pollutants. According to the EPA's website, ozone "can trigger a variety of health problems including chest pain, coughing, throat irritation, and congestion. It can worsen bronchitis, emphysema, and asthma."

The negative health effects of ethanol-blended gasoline have placed the EPA in the odd position of enforcing rules that run directly counter to its stated goals. On its website, the agency says that "reducing emissions of NO$_x$ is a crucial component of EPA's strategy for cleaner air." Nevertheless, when asked about the higher emissions related to ethanol, EPA spokesperson Jennifer Wood insisted that they are "very minimal increases." She also told me that the agency has other "tools under the Clean Air Act to reduce NO$_x$."

Wood's claim leaves clean air advocates like William Becker of the National Association of Clean Air Agencies gasping. He said the EPA is "scoffing at a 4 to 7 percent increase in air emissions at a time when agencies across the country would do anything to achieve that kind of a reduction in VOCs and NO$_x$." Becker's Washington-based group represents the interests of air pollution control authorities from 49 of the 50 states and several territories, as well as local agencies from 165 metro areas around the U.S. He said the pollution increases admitted by EPA are "a significant amount of emissions in any location in this country. And we can't just willy nilly be giving it away, particularly when states are struggling to meet current ozone standards."

The EPA's ethanol fact sheet infuriates Debbie Cook, mayor pro tem of Huntington Beach, a city located west of Los Angeles that struggles with air-quality problems. "The EPA's air quality rules in Southern California are largely a joke," Cook told me shortly after the EPA announcement. And the agency's April 10 [2007] statement touting ethanol, she says, "makes the joke worse."

It's not just the EPA that says ethanol is bad for air quality. Numerous studies have reached the same conclusion.

In 2004, the California Air Resources Board released a study saying that gasoline containing ethanol caused VOC emissions to increase by 45 percent when compared to pure gasoline. In 2006, the South Coast Air Quality Management District—the agency that oversees air quality issues for some 15 million people living in or near Los Angeles County—determined that gasoline containing 5.7 percent ethanol may add as much as 70 tons of VOCs per day to the state's air. This means that the Los Angeles area alone would account for about 25,500 tons of additional volatile organic compounds per year—or more than half of the minimum amount (41,000 tons) estimated by the EPA in its April 10 fact sheet.

[In] April [2007], Mark Z. Jacobson, an engineering professor at Stanford University, published a study concluding that the widespread use of E85 (fuel that contains 85 percent ethanol and 15 percent gasoline) "may increase ozone-related mortality, hospitalization, and asthma by about 9 percent in Los Angeles and 4 percent in the United States as a whole" when compared to the use of regular gasoline. Jacobson also found that because of its ozone-related effects, E85 "may be a greater overall public health risk than gasoline."

The Grocery Tax

While Americans are breathing more polluted air due to ethanol, they are also paying more at the grocery store, a fact that leads to the fourth problem: ethanol is increasing food prices.

[In June 2007], researchers from Iowa State University's Center for Agricultural and Rural Development released a report that looked at how ethanol production—which consumed 20 percent of America's corn crop in 2006—is affecting overall food prices. They found that increased ethanol production has resulted in higher prices on a panoply of foods, including: cheese, ice cream, eggs, poultry, pork, cereal, sugar, and beef. The researchers reported that between July 2006 and May 2007, the food bill for every American has increased by about $47 as a result of surging prices for corn and the associated price increases of other grains like soybeans and wheat. In aggregate, they concluded that American consumers will face a "total cost" for ethanol "of about $14 billion."

Let's put that $14 billion in perspective. [In 2006], the U.S. produced five billion gallons of ethanol. That means that Americans are effectively paying a new tax (in the form of higher food costs) of nearly $3 for each gallon of ethanol produced. And that doesn't count any of the subsidies for corn production mentioned above or the 51-cents-per-gallon federal tax credit given to companies that blend ethanol into gasoline. Worse yet, it's not just Americans who are being fleeced. The Iowa State researchers determined that, thanks to ethanol's voracious appetite for grain, "the rest of the world's consumers [will] also see higher food prices."

Iowa Rules

Given the many problems associated with ethanol (this story provides a partial list), why are members of Congress and presidential candidates eager to embrace it? Why has such an expensive, polluting, fuel become what one critic calls "the ag-ricultural equivalent of holy water?" There are two plausible explanations: the value of empty—but appealing—political rhetoric; and the Iowa Imperative.

[Ethanol is] bad for taxpayers, bad for air quality, bad for people who like to eat, and it will have no real effect on America's overall energy mix.

Ethanol boosters claim that ethanol is part of the prescrip-tion for energy independence—a concept that polls extremely well. The idea of energy independence appeals to a wide range of voters from the left and the right. The result: almost any-thing that promises to move America toward that goal—a goal that is neither achievable nor desirable because of the enormous costs it would entail—quickly garners wide support and massive subsidies.

Second, it's about Iowa, America's leading ethanol pro-ducer. Any candidate who wants to win the White House must have a good showing in the Iowa caucuses, which will be held January 14 [2008]. The numbers explain the imperative: Since 2002, the amount of Iowa corn going into ethanol pro-duction has tripled. The state now has some 21 ethanol plants and another 23 either planned or under construction. About 2,500 jobs are directly related to ethanol production and an-other 14,000—according to IowaCorn.org—are "affected" by ethanol. Those jobs are supported by huge federal subsidies. In 2005 alone, according to the Environmental Working Group, Iowa got $1.8 billion in corn subsidies—about $608 for every Iowan.

Given those numbers, it's hardly surprising that a January 2007 poll found that 92 percent of Iowa voters believe ethanol is important to the state's economic future. That explains why "when politicians come to Iowa, they have to say ethanol is great," says Iowa State University political science professor

Steffen Schmidt. Alas, what makes the ethanol business great for 3 million Iowans is bad for 297 million other Americans: It's bad for taxpayers, bad for air quality, bad for people who like to eat, and it will have no real effect on America's overall energy mix.

Aside from those little quibbles, ethanol truly is a miracle potion.

14

Energy-Efficient Transportation Can Reduce America's Foreign Oil Dependence

Chris Wolf

Chris Wolf is the president of Americans for Energy Independence, an organization that seeks to educate the public on the dangers of being dependent on other countries for energy.

The Iraq Study group concluded that U.S. interests in Middle Eastern oil creates distrust and causes other countries to be wary of our efforts to promote democracy in the region. The high financial and political costs of the Iraq war highlight the importance of reducing our dependence on Middle Eastern oil. The quickest way to do this is by reducing the amount of energy used for transportation.

The Iraq Study Group just released their report and as expected the report paints a very bleak picture of the situation on the ground and our prospects for success. On top of this, total expenditures for this campaign are now cresting $400 billion and our weekly run rate is estimated at $2 billion dollars! While our Army is at war, the majority of the American people have yet to participate or sacrifice in any way. Worse, our government has decided to borrow money to pay for the war versus asking you and me to foot the bill. Of course the bill will come due, but we'll let future generations figure out how to pay off our massive $9 trillion dollar national debt.

Chris Wolf, "Pay Me Now or Pay Me Later—Iraq and Oil," *Americans for Energy Independence*, December 7, 2006. Reproduced by permission.

While the charter of the Iraq Study Group was to find a way out of the current quagmire, they failed to address one of the primary drivers for why that part of the world is so critically important to U.S. interests in the first place—oil. Can any government or power base in Iraq or anywhere in the Middle East trust our motives when we are so dependent upon a resource in which they have 75% of the world's known reserves?

Of course not, especially given our 50 year history of intervening in the region to protect our "strategic interests". The Iraq Study Group report states: "Most of the region's countries are wary of U.S. efforts to promote democracy in Iraq and the Middle East." The current war and our past forays are exactly why we need to make Middle East oil strategically irrelevant.

As we drive around our gas guzzlers with yellow "support the troops" ribbons, we fail to see, or worse, we refuse to see that our own behaviors are driving our government's actions and indirectly aiding our enemies. We now consume over 130 billion gallons of gasoline each year, which comes from 7.3 billion barrels of oil, nearly 60% of which is imported. Twenty-two percent of the world's oil is in the hands of state sponsors of terrorism and under U.S./UN sanctions, and this does not include Saudi Arabia. Our intelligence community has already gone on record stating that wealthy individuals from Saudi Arabia, UAE [United Arab Emirates] and Kuwait (our allies in the region) have been funneling money to insurgents in Iraq and to terrorist organizations around the world.

There are no silver bullets that will end our Middle East oil dependence overnight. We do know that the only area where we can make quick and sudden reductions in oil consumption is in the transportation sector. This means using less gasoline—period. If you research the U.S. energy situation, you will see that the transportation sector not only ranks the highest in oil consumption but it is also on an out-of-control growth trajectory.

What Can We Do?

Proactively, Americans can decide to:

a) use public transportation or bicycle,

b) drive less by consolidating trips and

c) buy a more fuel efficient vehicle for your daily commute

We purchase 16 million new passenger vehicles annually, which relates to replacing 7% of the U.S. fleet of 200 million passenger vehicles every year. If we strive to improve our fuel efficiency by 20% every time we go to buy our next car, we can radically impact our oil consumption in as little as 5 years.

What Should We Ask Our Elected Representatives to Do?

Legislatively, our new congress needs to:

a) update the 30 year old CAFE [Corporate Average Fuel Economy] standards for vehicle fuel efficiency and eliminate the loop holes for light trucks and SUVs,

b) add a dollar "war tax" to each gallon of gasoline

c) make all Department of Transportation funds going to states contingent upon their adopting vehicle registration fees tied to fuel efficiency

The gasoline "war tax" would generate over $130 billion dollars per year. This would enable us to pay the current $2 billion per week the war is costing us and we would have enough left over to start paying down the $400 billion dollars this war has added to our national debt. Even with this tax, it would take us 13 years to pay off the $400 billion and that's without adding in the interest!

Ouch. Yes, this tax would hurt every time we fill up our vehicles. The value of this tax is that it gets all Americans to shoulder some of the pain associated with the war effort and it would drive us to make vehicle fuel efficiency a top personal priority.

Only by slowing and reversing our nation's demand for oil can we reestablish our nation's foreign policy reputation. Lowering oil demand in the transportation sector is the only short-term solution that can yield measurable results, and individual Americans can decide to do this even before we have a much needed national energy strategy.

In November [2006], voters showed Washington that the status quo of the Iraq war was no longer acceptable. The question remains as to the average American's willingness to sacrifice in order to truly support our troops and to help pay for the war effort now versus leaving this to our children to worry about later.

Organizations to Contact

The editors have compiled the following list of organizations concerned with the issues debated in this book. The descriptions are derived from materials provided by the organizations. All have publications or information available for interested readers. The list was compiled on the date of publication of the present volume; the information provided here may change. Be aware that many organizations take several weeks or longer to respond to inquiries, so allow as much time as possible.

American Council for an Energy-Efficient Economy (ACEEE)
1001 Connecticut Ave. NW, Suite 801
Washington, DC 20036
(202) 429-8873 • fax: (202) 429-2248
e-mail: info@aceee.org
Web site: www.aceee.org

ACEEE actively participates in the energy debate, developing policy recommendations and documenting how energy efficiency measures can reduce energy use, air pollutant emissions, and greenhouse gas emissions while benefiting the economy. ACEEE publishes technical reports, consumer guides, and books.

The Brookings Institution
1775 Massachusetts Ave. NW, Washington, DC 20036
(202) 797-6000 • fax: (202) 797-6004
e-mail: communications@brookings.edu
Web site: www.brookings.edu

The Brookings Institution is a private nonprofit organization devoted to conducting independent research and developing solutions to complex domestic and international problems. Brookings's goal is to provide high-quality analysis and recommendations for decision-makers on the full range of challenges facing an increasingly interdependent world. The organization publishes books, reports, and journals, including the *Brookings Review*.

Center for Strategic & International Studies (CSIS)
1800 K St. NW, Washington, DC   20006
(202)887-0200 • fax: (202) 775-3199
e-mail: webmaster@csis.org
Web site: www.csis.org

The Center for Strategic and International Studies partners with government to conduct research and develop policy solutions in areas of strategic interest, including defense and security policy, global policy and regional transformation. CSIS publishes books, reports, and newsletters, available on its Web site.

Council on Foreign Relations
The Harold Pratt House, New York, NY   10065
(212) 434-9400 • fax: (212) 434-9800
e-mail: webmaster@cfr.org
Web site: www.cfr.org

The Council on Foreign Relations is a nonpartisan think tank and publisher. It publishes briefing materials and research reports for government officials, business executives, journalists, educators, and other concerned citizens on a range of foreign policy issues, including national security, energy, economics, and the environment.

National Commission on Energy Policy
1225 Eye St. NW, Suite 1000, Washington, DC   20005
(202) 637-0400 • fax: (202) 637-9220
e-mail: info@energycommission.org
Web site: www.energycommission.org

The National Commission on Energy Policy is a bipartisan organization that conducts research on the rapidly changing landscape of energy needs, vulnerabilities, and opportunities, with the aim of strengthening the economy, safeguarding national security, and protecting the global environment and public health.

Natural Resources Defense Council

40 W. Twentieth St., New York, NY   10011
(212) 727-2700 • fax: (212) 727-1773
e-mail: nrdcinfo@nrdc.org
Web site: www.nrdc.org

The Natural Resources Defense Council is an environmental action organization. Its Web site includes policy reports on a variety of issues, including alternative energy sources and energy and the environment.

New America Foundation

1630 Connecticut Ave. NW, 7th Fl., Washington, DC   20009
(202) 986-2700 • fax: (202) 986-3696
Web site: www.newamerica.net

The New America Foundation sponsors a wide range of research, writing, and educational events and public outreach on important global and domestic issues such as energy and the environment, foreign policy, trade, and globalization. The foundation publishes articles, policy papers, and books, available on its Web site.

RAND Corporation

Office of Community Relations
Santa Monica, CA   90407-2138
(310) 393-0411, x7517
e-mail: Iao_Katagiri@rand.org
Web site: http://rand.org

The RAND Corporation is a nonprofit research organization that performs policy analysis on critical political and economic issues such as energy and environment, international affairs, terrorism, and homeland security. RAND publishes reports, research briefs, and books, available on its Web site.

U.S. Department of Energy (DOE)

1000 Independence Ave. SW, Washington, DC   20585
(800) 342-5363 • fax: (202) 586-4403

e-mail: the.secretary@hq.doe.gov
Web site: http://energy.gov

The Department of Energy's mission is to advance the national, economic, and energy security of the United States; to promote scientific and technological innovation; and to ensure environmental cleanup of the national nuclear weapons complex. The DOE Web site publishes the National Energy Policy, as well as information on ongoing policy initiatives and issues affecting energy security and the economy.

The White House
1600 Pennsylvania Ave. NW, Washington, DC   20500
(202) 456-1414 • fax: (202) 456-2461
e-mail: comments@whitehouse.gov
Web site: http://whitehouse.gov

The White House is the home and office of the president of the United States and his Council of Economic Advisors. The White House Web site provides general information on the energy policy, national security, and the environment.

Yale Center for the Study of Globalization
PO Box 208360, New Haven, CT   06520-8360
(203) 432-1900 • fax: (203) 432-1200
e-mail: globalization@yale.edu
Web site: www.ycsg.yale.edu

The Yale Center for the Study of Globalization was founded in 2001 to enrich debate between Yale University and the policy-making world on issues of globalization, including trade, security and terrorism, and the economy. The organization's on-line magazine, *YaleGlobal*, publishes articles on a range of issues and archives relevant academic papers that explore the impact of globalization on cultures and economies.

Bibliography

Books

Robert Baer

Sleeping with the Devil: How Washington Sold Our Soul for Saudi Crude. New York: Crown, 2003.

James Addison Baker, Lee Hamilton, and Lawrence S. Eagleburger

The Iraq Study Group Report. New York: Vintage, 2006.

James T. Bartis, Tim Latourrette, D. J. Peterson, and Gary Cecchine

Oil Shale Development in the United States: Prospects and Policy Issues. Rand, 2005.

Pierre Chomat

Oil Addiction: The World in Peril. Boca Raton, FL: Universal, 2004.

John M. Deutch and James R. Schlesinger

The National Security Consequences of U.S. Oil Dependency: Report of an Independent Task Force. New York: Council on Foreign Relations, 2006.

Emirates Center for Strategic Studies and Research

Gulf Oil in the Aftermath of the Iraq War: Strategies and Policies. Abu Dhabi,UAE: Emirates Center for Strategic Studies and Research, 2005.

Stephen E. Flynn

The Edge of Disaster: Rebuilding a Resilient Nation. New York: Random House, 2007.

S. David Freeman   *Winning Our Energy Independence.* Layton, UT: Gibbs Smith, 2007.

Michael T. Klare   *Blood and Oil: The Dangers and Consequences of America's Growing Petroleum Dependency.* New York: Metropolitan Books, 2004.

Nikolas Kozloff   *Hugo Chavez: Oil, Politics and the Challenge to the United States.* New York: Macmillan, 2006.

Leonardo Maugeri   *The Age of Oil: The Mythology, History and Future of the World's Most Controversial Resource.* Westport, CT: Praeger, 2006.

T. Christian Miller   *Blood Money: Wasted Billions, Lost Lives, and Corporate Greed in Iraq.* New York: Little, Brown, 2006.

Kevin P. Phillips   *American Theocracy: The Peril and Politics of Radical Religion, Oil, and Borrowed Money in the 21st Century.* New York: Viking, 2006

Stephen J. Randall   *United States Foreign Oil Policy Since World War I: For Profits and Security.* Montreal: McGill-Queen's University Press, 2005.

Paul Roberts   *The End of Oil: On the Edge of a Perilous New World.* Boston: Houghton Mifflin, 2004.

David Sandalow   *Freedom from Oil: How the Next President Can End the United States' Oil Addiction.* New York: McGraw-Hill, 2008.

Vijay V. Vaitheeswaran	*Power to the People: How the Coming Energy Revolution Will Transform an Industry, Change Our Lives, and Maybe Even Save the Planet.* New York: Farrar, Straus & Giroux, 2003.
Christine Woodside	*The Homeowner's Guide to Energy Independence: Alternative Power Sources for the Average American.* Guilford, CT: Lyons, 2007.
Daniel Yergin	*The Prize: The Epic Quest for Oil, Money, and Power.* New York: Simon & Schuster, 1991.
Abdulhay Y. Zalloum	*Oil Crusades: America Through Arab Eyes.* London: Pluto, 2007.

Periodicals

Philip E. Auerswald	"The Irrelevance of the Middle East," *American Interest*, Summer 2007.
Philip E. Auerswald	"The Myth of Energy Insecurity," *Issues in Science and Technology*, Summer 2006
Andrew J. Bacevich	"Breaking the Habit: How the U.S. Traded Freedom for Oil," *Commonweal*, March 10, 2006.
Gawdat Bahgat	"Oil and Militant Islam: Strains on U.S.-Saudi Relations," *World Affairs*, Winter 2003.

Ronald Bailey — "Feed SUVs and Starve People? Why Turning Food into Fuel May Not Be Such a Good Idea," *Reason*, June 22, 2007.

Marcia Merry Baker — "Biofuels Are Famine Policy; Food Shortages Are Hitting," *Executive Intelligence Review*, June 8, 2007.

Tsvi Bisk — "The Energy Project: Independence by 2020; Breaking Free from Oil Imports Is Critical for World Peace. Here's How It Will Be Done," *Futurist*, January-February 2007.

"Dennis Blair and Kenneth Lieberthal — 'Smooth Sailing: The World's Shipping Lanes Are Safe," *Foreign Affairs*, June 2007.

Keith A. Butler — "Develop Drilling in Alaska to Aid Energy Independence," *Detroit News*, October 23, 2007.

Frank Davies — "Moving at a Glacial Pace on Energy," *San Jose (CA) Mercury News*, October 16, 2007.

Denver Post — "U.S. Needs Energy Plan, Not Politics," August 2, 2007.

Murray Evans — "Ex-CIA Chief Wants Energy Independence," *Associated Press*, October 18, 2007.

Bill Farren-Price — "For Oil Producers, Energy Security Rises Up the Political Agenda," *International Herald-Tribune*, October 28, 2007.

John Fialka   "Energy Independence: A Dry Hole?" *Wall Street Journal*, July 5, 2006.

Thomas L. Friedman   "The New Red, White and Blue," *New York Times*, January 6, 2006.

David L. Goldwyn and Ian Perry   "Energy and Security," *Issues in Science and Technology*, Fall 2006.

David D. Hale   "Commodities, China and American Foreign Policy: How All Are Linked," *International Economy*, Summer 2006.

Victor Davis Hanson   "How Oil Lubricates Our Enemies," *American Enterprise*, July-August 2006.

Antonio Juhasz   "Mission Iraqi Oil: The Bush–Big Oil Scheme to Obtain Iraqi Petroleum Reserves," *Multinational Monitor*, January 2007.

Jan H. Kalicki   "Rx for Oil Addiction: The Middle East and Energy Security," *Middle East Policy*, Spring 2007.

Leonardo Maugeri   "Two Cheers for Expensive Oil," *Foreign Affairs*, March-April 2006.

Julia Nanay   "Oil Titans: National Oil Companies in the Middle East," *Middle East Policy*, Fall 2007.

Marc V. Schanz   "The Fuel War," *Air Force Magazine Online*, June 2007.

Steve Stein   "Breaking the Oil Habit," *Policy Review*, August-September 2006.

James Strock   "The Cure for Oil Addiction Is Leadership," *Futurist*, January-February 2007.

Matthew L. Wald   "The Long Road to Energy Independence," *New York Times*, January 28, 2007.

Ron Wiggins   "Only Our Energy Independence Wins World War on Terrorism," *Palm Beach (FL) Post*, March 11, 2004.

Fareed Zakaria   "Mile by Mile, into the Oil Trap," *Washington Post*, August 23, 2005.

Index

A

Air quality issues, ethanol, 81–83
Al Qaeda, 12–13
Alternative energy subsidies, 35
Alvarez, Bernardo, 48–52
Arctic National Wildlife Refuge
    (ANWR), 12–13, 37–38
Automakers
    energy policy and, 16–17
    FFVs and, 19, 27, 31
    fuel-efficient cars by, 15–16,
        29–30

B

Big Five oil companies, 54
Bin Laden, Osama, 12
Biofuels
    Brazil and, 16, 50, 73–74
    commercialization of, 30
    energy policy and, 16–18
    See also Ethanol
Brazil, 16, 38–39, 50, 73–74
Bryce, Robert, 76–85
Bush, George W., 7–8
    energy bill and, 14, 23
    energy independence stance
        of, 14, 33
    energy policy and, 14
    ethanol, no contribution to
        energy independence by,
        76–77
    fuel efficiency standards of,
        14, 25–26
    Iraqi oil stance and, 53, 59
    oil addiction of, 22–23
    oil dependence and, 42

    renewable fuel funding and,
        14, 15
    Twenty in Ten goal and,
        24–26

C

CAFE. See Corporate Average Fuel
    Economy
California Air Resources Board, 82
California Department of Trans-
    portation (CalTrans), 73
Carbon emissions, coal-based,
    67–69
Carbon storage, underground, 68
Carter, Jimmy, 26, 67
Cellulosic ethanol, 24–25, 30, 80
China, 13, 17, 61
Clean and Green Fleet plan, 29
Clinton, Bill, 7, 80
Clinton, Hillary, 54
Coal, as environmental threat
    OPEC, 67
    U.S. Air Force, 67
Coal, liquified, 67–68
Coal, role in U.S. energy self-
    reliance
        lack of U.S. refinery capacity,
            63–64
        Thomas, Craig (U.S. Senator),
            63–65
        U.S. national energy policy
            and, 64
        vs. ethanol, 64–65
Coal-based energy, as environ-
    mental threat
        carbon emissions and, 67–69
        congressional proponents of,
            69

liquefaction expense and, 70
as liquid fuel, 67–68
underground carbon storage of, 68

Coal-liquification expense, 70

Coal-to-Liquids Coalition, 68–70

Congressional proponents, coal-based energy, 69

Consumption gap, Western Hemisphere, 49–50

Corn-based ethanol, 24–25

Corn subsidies, 78

Corporate Average Fuel Economy (CAFE), 19, 88

D

Dalmia, Shikha, 8–9, 44–47

Department of Defense (DoD), 7, 18

Drilling, domestic, 37–38

E

E85 fuel blends/pump
energy policy, 18–20
ethanol contribution to, 72–75, 82–83
five-point energy independence plan, 30
fuel station infrastructure, 73–74
production technology, 74–75
strategic energy solution, 72

Edwards, John, 77

Electric transportation, 31–32
See also Hybrid vehicles

Energy bill, 14, 23

Energy-efficient transportation solutions, individual, 88

Energy imports, 25

Energy independence, achievable goal
Bush, George W., 14
Clean and Green Fleet plan, 29
Feldman, Rich, 27–32
five-point energy independence plan for, 29–32
Mazza, Patrick, 27–32
25x25 movement and, 28
for Washington (state), 27–32

Energy independence, misguided/unrealistic goal
alternative energy subsidies of, 35
Bush, George W., 33
domestic drilling of, 37–38
energy self-reliance of, 34–35
ethanol costs and, 38–39
ethanol fossil-fuel requirements and, 39
greenhouse gases and, 37
influence on U.S. oil companies and, 36
political/media support and, 34
realistic need for, 36–37
Seymour, Julia A., 33–39
taxpayer costs on, 35–36
U.S. oil import sources and, 35
Yergin, Daniel, 34–35

Energy policy, as key
ANWR, 12–13
automakers, 16–17
bin Laden, Osama, 12
biofuels, 16–18
Bush, George W., 14
CAFE, 19
China, 17
commitment to, 15–16
E85 fuel blend, 18–20
Energy Security Director, 20

ethanol, 18
fuel economy standards, 16–17
fuel-efficient cars, 15–16
global warming, 12
government role in, 18–19
health care costs and, 17
Health Care for Hybrids, 17
Japan, 16
nuclear program, Iran, 13
Obama, Barack, 11–21
oil as weapon, 13–14
oil pipeline attacks, Nigeria, 13
oil refinery attack, Al Qaeda, 12–13
renewable fuel market, 19–20
Saudi Royal Family, 11
Energy policy, government interference
Carter, Jimmy, 26
cellulosic ethanol, 24–25
corn-based ethanol, 24–25
federal constraints, 22
FFVs, 27
fossil fuels, 23
free-market energy policy, 26
fuel economy standards, 25–26
hybrid vehicles, 25
Lieberman, Ben, 22–26
oil/natural gas production, domestic, 23
performance-based transportation policy, 23
Reagan, Ronald, 26
renewable fuels mandate, 24
urban traffic congestion, 23
Energy security
Energy Security Director and, 20
Iraq infrastructure and, 61–62
national implications of, 7

oil dependence, non-threat to, 44–47
problems, Iraq, 58
U.S. energy policy and, 53–54
Venezuela, key to U.S., 48–52
Energy Security Director, 20
Energy Technology Program proposal, 18
Environmental Protection Agency (EPA), 80–82
EPA. *See* Environmental Protection Agency
Ethanol
Brazil subsidies, 38–39
cellulosic, 24–25, 30, 80
corn-based, 24–25
costs of, 38–39
energy imports on, 25
as energy policy, 18
fossil-fuel requirements, 39
fuel economy, 11
problems as gasoline/diesel substitute, 65
vs. coal, 64–65
Ethanol, contribution to energy independence
CalTrans, 73
corn issues, 74
E85 fuel blends/pump, 72–75
FFVs, 71–73
GM strategy, 71–73
Makower, Joel, 71–75
U.S. Energy Department and, 74–75
Ethanol, non-contribution to energy independence
air quality issues, 81–83
Bryce, Robert, 76–85
Bush, George W., 76–77
California Air Resources Board, 82
cellulosic, 80

corn subsidies, 78
E85 fuel blends/pump, 82–83
Edwards, John and, 77
effect on food prices, 82
EPA reports on, 80–82
insufficient production of, 79–81
Iowa production/economic effects pf, 83–85
McCain, John, 77
nitrogen oxide, 81–82
political motivations, 84
Renewable Fuel Standard, 80
subsidy requirements, 77–79
VOCs, 81–82

F

Federal constraints, domestic oil reserves, 22
Feldman, Rich, 27–32
FFVs. *See* flex-fuel vehicles
Five-point energy independence plan
    biofuel commercialization and, 30
    E85 fuel blends/pump based on, 30
    electric transportation, 31–32
    fuel-efficient vehicle promotion, 29–30
    oil-crop growth, 30–31
    oil savings goal, 29
    transit-oriented development, 30
Flex-fuel vehicles (FFVs)
    in energy policy, 27
    ethanol in, 71–73
    legislation for, 19
    plug-ins, 31
Food prices, effect of ethanol, 82
Fossil fuels, 23, 39
Free-market energy policy, 26

Free-market vs. government energy policy, 42–43
Friedman, Thomas L., 9–10
Fuel economy/efficiency
    energy policy, as key to, 16–17
    ethanol, 11
    government interference with, 25–26
    standards for, 15
Fuel-efficient cars, automakers, 15–16, 29–30

G

Gasoline/diesel substitute, ethanol, 65
General Motors (GM), 71–73
Global oil market/trends, 41–42, 44–45
Global social/economic development, energy needs, 48–49
Global warming, 12, 31, 66, 69–70
Government energy policy vs. free-market, 42–43
Greenhouse gases, 37, 74
Greenspan, Alan, 28
Gregoire, Christine (governor), 28

H

Health care costs, 17
Health Care for Hybrids, 17
Holmquist, Jenea (state representative), 28
House Select Committee on Energy Independence and Global Warming, 66
Hurricane Katrina, 12
Hybrid vehicles, 15–16, 25, 31, 72
Hydrocarbon law, proposed, 54–56

I

Infrastructure security, Iraq, 61–62
International oil markets, 9
Iowa, ethanol
    economic effects, 84
    production, 83–85
Iran, 13, 44, 46–47
Iraq Study Group, 86–87
Iraqi oil, case against U.S. control
    Bush, George W., 53
    hydrocarbon law, proposed, 54–56
    Iraq war and, 53–54
    Landay, Jerry M., 53–56
    U.S. energy security policy of, 53–54
Iraqi oil development, U.S. involvement
    Bush, George W., 59
    infrastructure security, 61–62
    Makovsky, Michael, 57–62
    multilaw hydrocarbon regime, 60
    oil production, 58–60
    oil revenue growth, 58–59
    security problems, 58
    technical expertise, 60–61
    training funds, 61
Islamism, 10

J

Japan, 16–17

K

Katrina (hurricane), 12
Kelley, P. X., 40–43
Kennedy, John F., 28

L

Landay, Jerry M., 53–56
Legislation, transportation energy-efficiency, 19, 88–89
Lieberman, Ben, 22–26
Liquefaction expense, coal, 70

M

Makovsky, Michael, 57–62
Makower, Joel, 71–75
Mazza, Patrick, 27–32
McCain, John, 77
Multilaw hydrocarbon regime, 60

N

National Renewable Energy Laboratory, 14
National security implications, 7
Natural gas production, domestic, 23
Nichols, Greg (Seattle mayor), 29
Nigeria, 9, 13
Nitrogen oxides, 81–82
Nivola, Pietro S., 8
Nuclear program, Iran, 13

O

Obama, Barack, 11–21
Oil
    addiction to, 22–23
    Big Five oil companies and, 54
    consumption reduction, 16
    federal constraints, domestic reserves, 22
    global market dependence on, 44–45
    international markets, 9
    pipeline attacks, Nigeria, 13
    production, domestic, 23

production stagnation, Iraq, 58–60

refinery attacks, Al Qaeda, 13

revenue growth, Iraq, 58–59

savings goal, 29

U.S. companies, 36

U.S. energy costs, 36

U.S. import sources, 35

U.S. reserves, 12

Venezuelan reserves, 49–50

as weapon, 13–14

See also Iraqi oil; case against U.S. control; Iraqi oil development; U.S. involvement

Oil-crop growth, 30–31

Oil dependence, non-threat to national security

Dalmia, Shikha, 44–47

global oil market, 44–45

Iran oil, sale needs, 46–47

OPEC, 45–46

price determination, 44

Oil dependence, threat to U.S. interests

Bush, George W., 42

global oil trends of, 41–42

government energy policy vs. free market, 42–43

Kelley, P. X., 40–43

Smith, Frederick W., 40–43

supply shortfall effect, 40

transportation sector, 42

Oil/natural gas production, domestic, 23

OPEC. *See* Organization of Petroleum Exporting Countries

Organization of Petroleum Exporting Countries (OPEC), 45–46, 67

P

Pelosi, Nancy (House speaker), 35–37, 66, 77

Petro programs, Venezuela, 50

Petrolism, 9

Plug-In Partners, 31

Plumer, Bradford, 66–70

Political motivations, ethanol, 84

Price determination, oil dependence, 44

Promoting Energy Independence and Security (White House), 8

R

Reagan, Ronald, 26

Renewable Fuel Standard, 80

Renewable fuels

funding of, 14–15

mandate, 24

market for, 19–20

Washington (state), 27–32

S

Saudi Arabia, 11, 13

Select Committee on Energy Independence and Global Warming, 66

Seymour, Julia A., 33–39

Smith, Frederick W., 40–43

State Electrified Transportation Task Force (Washington), 31

Subsidy requirements, ethanol production, 77–79

Supply shortfall effect, oil, 40

Syn-fuels program, 24

T

Taxpayer, energy independence cost, 35–36

Technical expertise, Iraq, 60–61

Thomas, Craig (U.S. Senator), 63–65

Training funds, Iraq, 61

Transit-oriented development, 30

Transportation, energy-efficiency
  CAFE standards, 88
  CalTrans, 73
  electric, 31–32
  individual solutions to, 88
  Iraq Study Group on, 86–87
  legislative solutions for, 19, 88–89
  State Electrified Transportation Task Force, 31
  Wolf, Chris, 86–89
Transportation policy, performance-based, 23
Transportation sector, oil dependence, 42
25x25 movement, 28
Twenty in Ten goal, 24–26

U

Union of Concerned Scientists, 29
United States (U.S.)
  Air Force, 7–8
  Department of Defense (DoD), 7, 18
  Energy Department, 74–75
  energy security policy, 53–54
  energy self-reliance, 63–65
  Iraqi oil, against control, 53–56
  Iraqi oil, involvement with, 57–62
  national energy policy, 64
  oil companies, 36
  oil dependence threat, 40–43
  oil import sources, 35
  oil reserves, 12
  refinery capacity, 63–64
  Venezuela, key to energy security, 48–52
Urban traffic congestion, 23

V

Venezuela, key to U.S. energy security
  Alvarez, Bernardo, 48–52
  consumption gap, Western Hemisphere, 49–50
  global social/economic development, 48–49
  Petro programs, 50
Venezuelan oil reserves, 49–50
Volatile organic compounds (VOCs), 81–82

W

War on Terror, 14, 41
Washington (state)
  five-point energy independence plan, 29–32
  renewable fuels, 27–32
  State Electrified Transportation Task Force, 31
Weapon, oil as, 13–14
Western Hemisphere consumption gap, 49–50
Wolf, Chris, 86–89
Wynne, Michael W., 7

Y

Yergin, Daniel, 34–35